))) hatherleigh

Hatherleigh Press is committed to preserving and protecting the natural resources of the earth. Environmentally responsible and sustainable practices are embraced within the company's mission statement.

Visit us at www.hatherleighpress.com and register online for free offers, discounts, special events, and more.

Backyard Farming: Home Harvesting
Text copyright © 2013 Hatherleigh Press

Library of Congress Cataloging-in-Publication Data is available upon request.
ISBN: 978-1-57826-463-6

Cover Design by DcDESIGN
Interior Design by Nick Macagnone

Printed in the United States
10 9 8 7 6 5 4 3 2 1

TABLE OF CONTENTS

••

INTRODUCTION

With almost any harvest, whether from the garden, raised livestock, hunting, fishing, or even wild crafting, food preservation has almost always been a part of the end process. From ancient times to the modern day, the techniques developed for preserving one's harvest are still being practiced, both in the home and in the commercial market.

Food preservation is in your life each and every day, even if you have never canned a vegetable or frozen a piece of meat in your life. If you have purchased food in a tin can you have purchased preserved food. Enjoyed any beef jerky lately? Bought jelly or jam? Prepared a box of pasta or frozen pizza? Each and every one of these examples employs a time-tested method of preserved food. Most people do not even give a thought as to the many ways that preserving food affects their lives each and every day, and this is mainly due to the fact that they did not preserve the food themselves.

However, with the rising return of home gardens, urban farms, homesteads, small farms, and even farmers' markets and roadside stands, this trend is changing. More and more households are turning once more to home preserving for their excess meat and produce.

In this book, we will begin by exploring a bit of the history of preserving food, and the ancient origins of some of the most common methods still being used today. Presented in an easy-to-understand and non-intimidating way, this book is your guide to rediscovering your roots through traditional, albeit updated, preservation techniques. Depending on what you plan on producing, you may want to try one, two, or all of the methods discussed.

The first step is to go through the methods. Decide which process is right for you or the particular food you are preserving, and dive in. Food preservation takes some time; but during the dead of winter, when the roads are covered in snow, and the last thing you want to do is head out to the store, you'll appreciate the foods that you "put up" from your harvest.

This book is meant to serve as a basic primer for those just beginning to keep and preserve their harvests. It is a short but concise book that will touch on all of the major methods available to new homesteaders to greatly extend the use and shelf life of their produce. So find a comfy seat, consider your harvest plans for the coming seasons, and start making your own preservation plans.

MEET THE EXPERT

Kim Pezza grew up among orchards and dairy and beef farms having lived most of her life in the Finger Lakes region of New York state. She has raised pigs, poultry and game birds, rabbits and goats, and is experienced in growing herbs and vegetables. In her spare time, Kim also teaches workshops in a variety of areas, from art and simple computers for seniors, to making herb butter, oils, and vinegars. She continues to learn new techniques and skills and is currently looking to turn her grandparents' 1800s farm into a small, working homestead.

CHAPTER 1

A BRIEF HISTORY OF PRESERVING FOODS

he act of preserving food is as old as civilization, and like many of the things we take for granted today, the methods of preservation were most likely first discovered by accident and/or trial and error.

Some of the methods that we still use today trace their origins all the way back to ancient times, where forms of fermentation, oil packing, pickling, salting, drying, and smoking were all practiced regularly. One of the earliest recorded examples of food preservation is from ancient Egypt and shows the drying of grains and its storage in sealed silos.

Besides the Egyptians, the Greeks, Romans, Sumerians, and Asians all used various techniques of food preservation, and stored their food in clay jars. Their use of preservation endured and evolved into methods that we still use today.

But why was food preservation developed to begin with? The need for preservation arose due to the fact that in some areas, the climate dictated when food could or could not be grown. In other areas, especially those subject to harsh weather, raising livestock could be difficult if done year-round; instead livestock were raised for most of the year and would be slaughtered before winter set in. In both scenarios, the fruits, vegetables, and meats preserved and put aside after the harvest had to take people through the hard months when fresh foods would not be available. And, as food begins to spoil right at harvest time, if the people were to survive the lean times of certain seasons (whether it be the cold snowy winters in some regions or extremely hot summers in others), they had to be able to keep their food from spoiling.

Preservation, when done properly, prevents the growth of bacteria, fungi, and other microorganisms that would otherwise render the food unfit for consumption. It also prevents foods such as meats from going rancid by slowing fat oxidation, while at the same time (usually) maintaining the nutritional value of the food, along with its taste and texture. We say usually here, because there are times when some foods are altered, sometimes drastically, through preservation. One example of this is the use of pickling to preserve vegetables.

Historically, the way food was preserved would depend on location and even culture. As a result, diets would often differ from place to place, even if their climates or growing conditions were similar.

For example, in early colonial America some of the commonly used methods of preservation were smoking, drying, salting, pickling, and jellying. Drying would be used primarily in the southern states or territories where sun and heat was plentiful and foods could dry thoroughly. In northern climates, by contrast, jellying and pickling were the methods of choice, simply due to the fact that drying wasn't a feasible alternative due to lack of necessary "sun time" needed to properly dry the foods.

Food Preservation Through the Years

Now let's take a quick look, historically speaking, at the methods used by early civilizations worldwide. Further along, we will take a closer look at these methods, all of which are still in use today.

Canning

When talking about preserving the harvest, one of the first methods of preservation you would probably think about is canning (especially if you grew up with the grandmother or mother who always had a pantry full of home-canned goods!)

Canning, like freezing, is actually one of the "newer" preservation methods. It was developed in France in the mid-1790s, after Nicholas Appert was asked by Napoleon to find a way of preserving food so that the army could carry food supplies with them. By 1806, the French Navy was using the canning method for meat, milk, fruits, and vegetables.

In 1810, the tin can was first used in England as a storage container. Then, in 1851, Raymond Chevalier Appert patented the pressure canner. This enabled canning at temperatures higher than 212°F.

Today we still home can, and while we may have developed a few more techniques to make our food storage even safer, canning hasn't changed all that much over the years.

Sugar

Sugar is another form of preservation. Today we use sugar primarily as the method to create jelly or jam. In early cultures either sugar or honey, another form of sugar, would be used. A common mixture of produce and preserve was fruit and honey.

The ancient Greeks would take quince that they had first slightly dried and tightly pack it into jars with honey. The ancient Romans improved upon this method by first cooking the quince and honey together before packing, creating more of a jelly or jam.

Jellies and jams were a form of fruit preservation that was used as an alternative when it was not possible to dry fruits. A good example would be in the northern states of colonial America, where drying fruits was not practical or efficient. In areas like these, jellies and jams allowed families to still have fruit in the snowy winters.

Freezing (and Refrigeration)

It probably goes without saying, but **freezing** (and refrigeration) was among the most climate/weather specific method of storing and preserving foods. In areas of extreme cold and those that had winter conditions during at least part of the year, ice, snow and cold streams were used to keep items cold or, depending upon temperature, frozen. Caves were also used for this purpose, and in later times, people would build cellars designed for cold storage. These cold storage rooms, which we would come to know as root cellars, could store food at temperatures between 30° and 40°F.

The root cellar would then be replaced by the ice house (in the US) where ice and food would be stored. After this, the ice house was replaced by the icebox, which basically served to bring the ice house into the kitchen.

Later in the 1800s, true refrigeration would appear, and by the late 1800s a man named Clarence Birdseye would discover a way of quickly freezing foods, changing the manner of cold storage of foods forever. His techniques would later build into the home freezer method that we heavily depend on today.

Drying

Drying is one of the oldest forms of preservation, and is probably the simplest method of keeping food longer. Widespread use of the technique goes back as far as 6000 B.C., and evidence of its use goes back even further, to 12,000 B.C. in the Middle East and western parts of Asia.

In ancient Rome, the Roman people enjoyed dried fruits. The Middle Ages employed the use of still houses, similar to what we would think of as a smokehouse today, as an alternative to sun drying.

This allowed foods to be dried in areas or regions that did not have enough sun for the natural drying process to take place. Fruits, vegetables, and herbs could be dried in this manner.

In colonial America, drying was used mainly in the South,

where heat and sunlight was plentiful for natural drying, although other areas may have been able to take advantage of some drying as well. For example, even in the north, herbs and flowers were hung out to dry, in either an out building or inside the home.

Europeans used the drying process for fish more than for other meats, especially in those regions where fish such as cod and haddock were the main meat consumed.

A couple interesting points on drying originate with the Indians in early America and have to do with pumpkins having been a staple in their diet. Not only was pumpkin dried and ground into flour to be stored for later use, the pumpkin was also dried in strips, then woven into mats. These mats were not to eat but rather to sit or sleep on. An unusual use, when we think of drying foods to eat!

As simple as drying is, the method does have its disadvantages. Drying will obviously change the texture and taste of food. A perfect example is beef jerky. Compare a strip of dried meat to a strip of regular cooked meat. The differences in looks and taste are quite apparent.

Finally, dried foods require proper storage. Dampness can ruin dried foods, causing mold and spoilage (which will be discussed further in Chapter 6).

Pickling

Pickling usually entails preserving food by immersing it in vinegar. One of the oldest forms of food preservation, it was made popular by the Romans, who used the technique of pickling fish to make something called garum, which was pickled fish sauce. Use of pickling rose during the sixteenth century due to the arrival of new foods in Europe and today is still one of the most well-known and popular forms of food preservation.

Curing

Although dehydration may be the earliest known form of **curing**, most people, when prompted, will probably first think of salt curing. Salt is one of the oldest known food additives. In 1250 B.C., during the time of the Phoenicians, fish were gutted, dried, and then packed in salt. In ancient Rome, the word "salary" came from the Roman word salarium (meaning "salt"). Salt was so important during this time that soldiers received salt as payment. The ancient Egyptians even use salt as part of their embalming process. The Middle Ages also found a great many uses for salt, particularly in curing their meat.

By the 1800s, the methods of using salt for curing were greatly improved when it was discovered that some salts work better with meats than others. It was noticed that some salts, when mixed with saltpeter, left the meats more red and pleasing in appearance. Foods that were preserved using these methods include pork, beef, and fish, foods that we continue to salt today.

Herring was (and still is) a common fish to be salted. The fish needed to be preserved quickly, as the oil of the fish goes bad, usually within 24 hours of the catch.

Smoking

As with drying, smoking as a preservation technique dates back to at least 6000 BC. Some believe that it was the still houses used for drying in the Middle Ages that had a part in making smoking popular as a method of preserving food. People discovered that the effects of the smoke on some of the foods that they were drying allowed them to create more flavorful and longer-lasting preserves in certain cases. Smoke houses were used in early times and were usually any type of shed or covered structure.

A sketch depicting members of the Timucua tribe drying food by smoking.

Fish was the first meat smoked, and there is evidence that in ninth century Poland, the technique was so popular that large quantities of fish were smoked for later consumption. In the late nineteenth century, smoked pork became a popular way for farmers in early America to preserve and store meat

Fish smoking in a homemade smoker.

from the fall/winter pig slaughter, as it allowed them to be able to keep the meat throughout the winter.

Smoking has become popular again today and is a form of food preparation particularly used for preserving meats.

Fermentation

Fermentation is another ancient form of preservation, possibly going back as far as 10,000 B.C. Some products that are made through fermenting are kimchi, sauerkraut, wine, and beer. Although you can certainly purchase foods preserved using a fermentation process; it is a process that is not commonly used in the average home today. However, this trend is changing as more and more households begin to prepare their own sauerkraut, beer, and wine at home.

This discussion is only a very brief look at the history of preserving methods. However, even this short glimpse is enough to show how long and storied the techniques of preserving food are. Most had very humble roots, but worked well enough that we still use the methods in one form or another today. In the next chapter, we will look at preserving for use in today's modern home.

CHAPTER 2

PRESERVING TODAY

· ·

Unlike during ancient times, in many societies we are no longer limited in our choices of preservation methods by the climate that we live in. Instead, we are able to choose the method that best fits our needs, tastes, time, and storage capabilities. Even drying can easily be done almost anywhere. If it can't be done by the sun, there are a number of ways available to us today; where once we needed to depend on the sun, now we can use generated heat instead to dry our foods.

You may have noticed that most of the methods discussed in Chapter 1 are methods that continue to be used today; some with minor changes, others with hardly any change at all. And added to this are the new methods that have joined the old: vacuum packaging and freeze-drying are both revolutionary techniques for preserving food for extended lengths of time (although freeze-drying is not commonly used when preserving at home).

Since almost any method of preservation you choose is available for use today how exactly do you narrow things down and select the correct method? The first thing that should be mentioned is that you do not have to restrict yourself to just one method. You also do not need to process your foods into just plain fruits, vegetables, or meats. For example: you may have many tomatoes from your harvest, but you really don't want 40 jars of preserved tomatoes on your pantry shelf? What do you do? Think about what you use those tomatoes for throughout the year, and plan your preservation accordingly. Do you use pasta sauce? If so, then take some of your tomatoes, make up a batch or two of sauce, and can or freeze it. Prefer salsa? Then take some of your tomatoes and make up a batch of salsa. If you use sun-dried tomatoes then you can dry some of your tomatoes, either in the sun, the oven, or dehydrator. Don't forget to save and can/freeze some whole tomatoes as well, to use for cooking.

Of course, if you are tight on time and just need to get your preserving done so you don't lose anything, you may end up with those 40 jars of tomatoes sitting on your shelf for a while, until you can put them into direct use. The point is that you have options, in both how you preserve foods and the method or methods you decide to use.

Selecting the Method for the Job

Since you have such a variety of food preservation methods available to you, how do you decide which one (or ones) to use? First, consider **your available resources.** If you are concerned about food being lost during a power failure or don't have a big freezer readily available, then freezing would be out. If you don't have lots of shelf space, it might make you think twice about canning. However, know that you can always store your jars in crates in the cellar or in a closet.

If you like to tent camp and/or hike, then you might consider drying and dehydrating food, this would create food requiring absolutely no refrigeration, as well as being easy to transport. Or, if you are preparing for Christmas gift giving, a combination of dehydrating, canning, and pickling could be the way for you to go.

The next thing you would want to look at is **what you are preserving.** You may love dried fruit, but don't want two or three bushels' worth. Although you could theoretically dry cucumbers, there isn't much call for its use, so with an overabundance of cucumbers, pickling may be the better answer.

Finally, you have to take into consideration **the equipment you have available.** For example, you can't smoke meat if you don't have a smoker or a grill, although you may be able to find a smokehouse nearby. If you want to dry foods, even without the sun or a dehydrator, you can still dry foods in either your oven or, to an extent, in the microwave as well.

Canning equipment is much easier to find now, and is available in many feed and farm stores, department stores, and through a number of online catalogues and suppliers. You may even be able to find jars and lids in grocery stores. You should also check your parents' or grandparents' cellar, attic, or garage for empty jars, especially if they used to can themselves.

Of course, you can always purchase the equipment needed for a project if you really have your heart set on a certain preservation technique, but that can get expensive depending on what you need. If you are on a budget you will probably need to select your method of preservation based on what equipment you have at your disposal and what you can reasonably afford.

The point is that while the resources available to you aren't necessarily subject to change, each act of preserving food is different, and the method chosen should be whichever is best suited.

Who Preserves Food

Today, people from all walks of life, incomes, and social statuses are practicing food preservation. And although home preserving may have fluctuated over the centuries, this is most likely the usual arrangement.

In ancient civilizations, it is likely that almost everyone did some type of preservation, as there was no refrigeration or freezing available to keep foods fresh (unless you lived in an area with winter snow and ice). In some of the more advanced ancient civilizations, where open markets were popular, some of the wealthier people may have purchased some of their foods preserved, and had their servants or cooks prepare the preserves.

In colonial America people preserved their harvests, including meats, in preparation for the harsh winters and resulting food shortages. Those who had funds and access would be able to purchase already preserved foods, and most likely did to an extent; meanwhile, kitchen servants would most likely prepare preserves as well.

Today, people are going back to basics and preserving their own foods again, in their homes. Because of the modern methods for transporting fresh produce, while they may be using fresh foods they have harvested themselves, they may also have received produce from friends or purchased it directly from the farmer. And unlike those who preserved their own foods throughout history, today's home food preservationist has a wide variety of equipment available to him/her to make their work easier. As stated before, we are not limited to area-specific preservation methods any longer, and we have a larger variety of foods available to us for preserving. As we aren't restricted to just the foods we harvest ourselves, the experience of preserving foods is not only much more interesting but much more fun.

The bottom line in figuring out which method(s) you're going to use in your journey through preservation is to first consider which methods will work best for you, and what kind of storage space you have. Don't forget that you will need to store everything you preserve somehow and somewhere. Think about how you will ultimately be using your preserved foods and then decide on your method from there.

The answer to the question of who preserves food today is a simple one. Although we have just discussed this a bit, there is one important person left off of the list: you! That's right; most likely, you have been practicing some sort of food preservation at home for years and just never realized it. Do you buy extra meat during a good sale and then bring it home and freeze it? Have you ever made jam? Even just using the packages for pickles or jelly (available in stores nowadays to make the work easier) counts as preserving food. If you have done anything like this, you have already been preserving and quite possibly never even given it a thought.

Preserving your harvest doesn't have to be complicated. It can be as simple as freezing some strawberries so that you can enjoy strawberry shortcake during the winter or turning some of your fresh ingredients into a prepared dish before canning, such as a vegetable soup. Once you get the hang of it, you'll be looking for new ways to preserve your foods…and maybe even new foods to preserve!

Creating a delicious pumpkin puree. Photo by Yoames under the Creative Commons Attribution License 2.0.

CHAPTER 3

THE HARVEST

· ·

Before you can think about preserving food, you'll first need food to preserve. Sure, it is an obvious statement, but it is the first step in the process. And there are certain steps to take during harvest to prepare your food for preservation. We will discuss the common processes in more detail in Chapters 4–9. Here, we will limit our discussion to the food itself and its preparation prior to preserving

Many who preserve food are doing so with food from their own harvest. Whether it is fruits, vegetables, herbs, or meat, individuals and families usually have enough to use both now and later on. So, let's start with the home garden harvest.

Cleaning Your Harvest

When you have harvested whatever was ready in your garden that day, the foods should first be cleaned. The way foods are cleaned depends on the food itself; foods that have had pesticides sprayed on them will need a more thorough cleaning than an organic food. Some foods will need a much gentler cleaning than others. For example, hard root vegetables will usually need a good scrubbing after harvesting simply due to the soil that will be clinging to them. You can take a little scrubber brush and clean under running water; however, to conserve water and prevent it from going down the sink drain, it is advisable to scrub the root vegetables first in a basin of water, and then quickly rinse in the sink of clean water.

With onions you may just be able to be gently wiped off of with a rag, as you need, at this point anyways, to be careful that you do not remove the paper skin; although, if one layer with all of the dirt comes off easily, that will clean the bulb up for you nicely. Garlic is the same way: just a light cleaning, so as to preserve the paper skin. Tomatillos may have the skin or husk totally removed, as you would not normally preserve the husk anyway.

Foods with either thin skin or no skin at all, like tomatoes, berries, apples, and plums, should be lightly washed and either gently dried or left to air dry. There is, however, one food that should not be washed, just gently wiped off, and that is mushrooms. If dropped into water or held under with running water, mushrooms will absorb the water like a sponge. So instead of washing a mushroom, just take a clean towel or napkin and gently wipe to remove any dirt. If the bottom of the stem is a little dirty after picking, it may be trimmed off.

At this point, you will have your foods washed and cleaned. Next you will need to get whatever equipment you'll need out and ready to use. (Again, this will be covered in more depth in Chapters 4–9.) From here, the food is prepared as per the recipe being used and the method of preservation being employed. For example, tomatoes would need to be peeled and seeded no matter what method is used. Vegetables or meats intended for dehydration need to be sliced according to the specifications of the dehydrator or the recipe. Fruits may need to be sliced, chunked, and so on. Again, at this stage your preparation depends on what you are doing.

After all the preparations are done, whatever you are pickling, drying, saucing, jamming, etc., those processes can be completed at this time. Finally, the method of storage will be chosen, the food packed away, and you will have finished your preserving.

Using Purchased Foods

But what if you don't have your own garden? Do you need to use fresh foods harvested "then and there?" The answer is no. That being said however, you will still need to be sure that the food you are preserving is as fresh as possible.

If you are purchasing from roadside stands, farm markets, or farmers markets, freshness is not usually a concern. If you're not sure how to tell if something is ripe enough for use, you can normally just ask somebody at the stand. In most cases, they will be more than happy to teach you how to tell if a fruit or vegetable is ripe enough for your needs. However, if purchasing from a grocery store, freshness may be a bit more of an issue. With the fact that many stores are now displaying most of their fruits and vegetables loose, it makes it that much easier to know what you are purchasing.

But for those that are still packaged, a bit more scrutiny is necessary. You need to watch for bad spots in your foods. Something like a potato can just have a bad spot cut from it before canning or freezing, but that same bad spot could have also affected others in the bag. If tomatoes are too old, even if it doesn't look too bad on the outside, it could end up fermenting in the jar, breaking the seal and spoiling the entire batch. (I myself have had this happen with my homegrown tomatoes when I held onto one batch a little too long before canning.) Once you are ready to can your store bought foods, your preparation and preservation process would be the same as it for your home harvest.

At this time, it would be worth mentioning that some foods can go bad rather quickly, such as tomatoes. If you are looking to can tomatoes, and you are aware that they could spoil quickly but just do not have the time to spend on canning, you can buy yourself some time by peeling, seeding, bagging, and then freezing the vegetables. Then, when you do have the time to can, you can begin the canning process. Note that this method will not work for everything (don't even try cucumbers) and if you want to use your tomatoes for a chunky salsa later, then freezing will not work either as the tomatoes will not be firm enough after thawing for making chunky salsa. But this will help you in salvaging at least some foods if you do not have time to can something right away before the harvest spoils.

What's Best for Preservation?

Not all foods preserve well with all methods, and in rare cases, some foods may only have one method that works well for their preservation. Although there are many recipes out there for the various preservation methods, sometimes you might just want to try something different and see if it works. And if so, go for it! Just remember that your experiment may not work out, and you'll have to throw away your efforts. That having been said, you might also create a wonderful preserve that you'll want to make again next year. And just in case that happens, you should really make notes of your procedure so that if it does become your foodie masterpiece you can make it again.

There is almost nothing that cannot be preserved in at least some way. Some foods may be limited in the methods that can be used to successfully preserve them, but you can usually find at least one way that will work. So now, let's take a more in-depth look at methods of preserving, the basic steps in using those methods and examples of what foods can be preserved with each technique.

CHAPTER 4

CANNING: JAMS, JELLIES, AND MORE

anning is the method everyone remembers seeing used in either their grandmother's or mother's kitchen. Canning may not be the fastest method of preservation, but once done (and done properly) you will have a shelf full of product that will need no refrigeration until opened. Canning is a great preservation method for those without large freezers and those who live in areas prone to power outages during storm seasons. For those choosing to live off the grid, with limited power capability, canning is practically essential.

A group of women at a food canning class

The equipment necessary for canning is basic, and although you may have a number of purchases to make the first time you can, most everything will be reusable for the next year's harvest.

Everything necessary to preserve with the canning method can be found quite easily in today's market. From farm stores to grocery stores, the home preserver can find whatever they need to accomplish their project. But that being said, what exactly will you need to do your canning? Let's look at the supply list.

(Note: As this book is written primarily for the beginner preserver, we will be focusing on the hot water bath form of canning. Although there is also the option of pressure canning, a method of canning similar to pressure cooking, the hot water bath method is the easiest method for the beginner, as well as for those who do not want to go to the expense of a pressure canner. We will discuss pressure canners only briefly.)

The Tools of the Trade

Let's first look at the equipment necessary for canning. While these items were once usually carried seasonally, many stores carry a small inventory year round.

Canning jars: Canning jars can be purchased in a number of places, from department stores to grocery stores. They come in half-pint, pint, and quart sizes, in wide mouth and regular sized jar openings, and are purchased by the box, with the quantity of jars per box depending on the jar size purchased. Sometimes these jars may be found at garage sales, secondhand stores, or even in the cellars of relatives. These jars may be reused from year to year. However, all jars, even if purchased new, should be checked for cracks and chips, especially around the opening. If there are any imperfections on the lip area of the jar, it will not seal properly, and it could cause the loss of the food in that particular jar, if it seals at all.

Lids and rings: These are the components that make up the jar covers. There are two sizes of lids and rings, with one size fitting wide mouth jar openings and the other size fitting the regular jar openings. Lids and rings may be purchased as sets or separately. Rings are reusable, but once lids are used they can no longer seal, cannot be reused, and must be thrown away.

Canner: This is the pot available to use the hot water bath canning method. The jars are placed within the pot of boiling water until they are ready to be pulled out of the hot bath. It should be noted that any non-reactive pot (stainless or enamel) that is deep enough to hold your jars and allow for 1 to 2 inches of water over the lid may be used, although canning kettles and pots can hold more jars than many other kettles and pots.

Canning basket: Although these are basically simple wire baskets, canning baskets can help keep the canning process safe. The filled jars are placed into the basket, which can then be plunged into and retrieved safely from the boiling water.

Canning funnel: A funnel with a wide opening to fit over the canning jars, which allows for easy filling. The opening into the jar is large enough to allow chunks or slices of fruits to pass through into the jars. Although not a necessity, the funnel does help keep messes to a minimum when filling jars. They will fit the half pint, pint, and quart jars, in both the wide mouth and regular sized varieties.

Magnetic lid wand: This is simply a plastic handle with a magnet on the end. However, the lid wand makes retrieving lids and rings out of the boiling water during the sterilization process much easier and safer.

Clean towels: Various sizes, depending on how many jars you are using. Some should be lint-free, while others may be the typical terrycloth type.

Clean knife, chopstick, or wooden skewer: This is to help release air from the jars before the lid is placed on it and it goes into the hot water bath. It is important that whichever instrument you elect to use is clean to prevent contamination of the food in the jar, which will lead to spoilage.

Permanent marker and labels: To mark and date jars before they are put on the shelf.

Jar lifter: Basically these are tongs for jars. The ends of the lifter are shaped to securely hold the jars by their top neck areas. The jar lifter can be used to lift hot jars in and out of the canner, and are useful even when a canning basket is used.

Canning supplies: jars, lids, and rings. Photo by Windell Oskay under the Creative Commons Attribution License 2.0.

Preparation of Jars, Lids, and Rings

Now that you have the equipment you need, it is time to prepare the jars, lids, and rings. They all need to be sterilized, but this is much easier than it sounds. Just add boiling water!

Basically, in order to sterilize the jars, lids, and rings, they just need to be boiled in water. This is done by simply placing the items in a large pot of boiling water on the stove. Do not microwave to a boil, as the lids and rings are metal. In addition, you would be at the jars all day, as you would only be able to microwave one or two jars at a time. Plus, you may not be able to get the water hot enough in a microwave. You can, however, use your canner to sterilize the jars.

With the canner sitting on the stove, stand the jars inside, right side up. Do not pack them in tightly. If you have a canning basket, you may sit the jars in the basket to sterilize. As you put the jars in the canner, carefully check the rims of the jar for nicks, chips, or cracks. Any jars that are found to be damaged should not be sterilized, and should instead be discarded.

Once the jars have been inspected and placed in the canner, it should be filled with hot water, to at least 1 inch over the top of the jars. Bring to a boil, and keep at a boil for at least ten minutes. If you are at an altitude above 1000 feet, add one minute per additional thousand feet. Turn off the heat and carefully remove the jars from the canner. Remember—the jars will have boiling water inside of them. Empty with extreme caution, and do not touch with your hands.

Carefully placing your jars in the canning basket will avoid any chipping. Illustration by Ariel Delacroix Dax.

While you are waiting for the jars to boil, spread one or two lint-free towels on a flat surface, like a countertop or table. The number of towels you will lay out depends on how many jars you will use.

Using a jar lifter to remove jars from the canner.

Once the jars are out and empty, stand them upside down on the lint-free towel. Let the jars sit until they are cool enough to handle. The jars may dry with a white film. This is normal; the jars will not need to be redone.

In the meantime, you will also need to boil and sterilize the lids and rings. This may actually be done in the same bath that the jars were sterilized in. Simply drop the lids and rings into the boiling

Jars in a canner full of boiling water. Photo by thebittenword.com under the Creative Commons Attribution License 2.0.

water and let boil, again for about ten minutes. Remove the lids and rings from the boiling water using the magnetic lid wand. Remember: the water is hot; therefore the rings and lids will be hot. Remove with caution.

Do not towel dry the jars, lids, or rings. Allow them to air dry. This eliminates the problem of any lint from the towels getting onto the jar, which if not caught could in turn cause the jars not to seal (if there is lint on the rim) or contaminate the food inside the jar (if lint is inside). As previously stated, while the jars dry they may have a white film on the outside. This is fine. After your canning is completed and the jars of food have been cooled, you may carefully clean up with a damp rag.

Once the jars, lids, and rings are sterilized and cool enough to handle so as not to get burned, they are now ready to fill with your prepared food. Note: it is sometimes said that the sterilization step may be skipped, as the jars will be sterilized during the actual canning process. I tend to take the attitude that this extra step can't hurt given how little time it takes, and it gives the jars an extra layer of clean. During the sterilization process, if you feel as though you are wasting a lot of water, when sterilization is completed and the water is no longer needed, carefully pour the water into a bucket and allow it to cool. Once cooled it is perfect for use on plants or gardens.

Filling the Jars

The foods that you choose should be prepared according to the recipe that you are using. When canning, it is important that everything is done properly to prevent contamination of foods, so do not cut corners.

When filling the jars, do so carefully. Jars should be filled to 1 inch from the top. If you are preparing something in a brine or juice, make sure that the food is covered by the liquid. For something like whole pickles or whole tomatoes, it is easier to pack directly into the jar; for other things like sauces, jellies, and pickle slices, it is easier and far less messy to fill the jars using the canning funnel.

Once the jars are full, using a plastic knife, wooden skewer, or chopstick, poke down the sides of the filled jar. You'll likely begin to see little bubbles come up the sides. This is releasing unwanted air. Continue until bubbles no longer appear. Wipe the rim of the jar with a damp, lint-free cloth to remove any brine, juice, or food that may have dripped onto it. If the jar isn't clean, then the jar will not seal. Once this is done, put on the lid and ring, placing the lid inside of the ring and screwing it onto the jar. The rubberized part of the lid should face down, so that when placed on the jar, the rubber is touching the glass rim. Make sure the lid is on firmly, but not as tight as to present difficulty in removing it

When filling jars, be sure to leave an inch of space to ensure a strong seal. Illustration by Ariel Delacroix Dax.

Make certain to wipe the rims of the jars to remove any excess, or the jars won't properly seal. Illustration by Ariel Delacroix Dax.

later. I usually turn the lid until hand tightened, and then do a light twist backwards. This will allow the lid to be on firmly but still allow easy removal later on.

Once the jars are covered, place them into the basket and lower them into the hot water in the canner. If you do not have a basket, carefully put the jars in the canner using your jar lifter. Water should be at least 1 inch over the top of the jars. Bring the water to a boil, leaving jars in the canner for the amount of time necessary for whatever food you are preserving. The chart below will give an idea of canning time for some items, while your recipes may give you further information.

Hot Water Bath Processing Times for High Altitude Locations

Feet	Increase in Processing Time
1,001 to 3,000 feet	5 minutes
3,001 to 6,000 feet	10 minutes
6,001 to 8,000 feet	15 minutes
8,001 to 10,000 feet	20 minutes

Note that the time can vary, especially depending on elevation. Use the times given as a starting point, and adjust as necessary for each batch.

While the jars are in the boiling water, you may hear some popping sounds. This is just the lids pulling in and sealing. These sounds are good. When it is time for the jars to come out, carefully set them on a towel-covered table or counter. Then cover jars with another towel and let sit and cool. Again, you may continue to hear the popping of the sealing lids. (Terry cloth towels are best for this. And if sitting on a wooden table or surface be sure that you have plastic under the

An assortment of preserved food in a pantry.

towels, so that the damp towels do not damage the wood finish.)

When the jars have cooled, remove the towel covering them. Test the lids. If you put your finger in the middle, is the lid firm and solid, or does it give and press down, then pop back up when you remove your finger? If it is solid, then the seal is good. If the lid pops up and down, it is not a good seal and will spoil quickly on the shelf. Should this happen, either put the jar in the fridge and use quickly or put the food into a freezer container and freeze. Do not put it on the shelf.

|||||||||||||||||||||||||||||||||||||||||||||||||||||||||||||||||||||||||||||||||||||

Pressure Canning

You may also choose to use the pressure canning method. This involves using a pressure canner (which is similar to a pressure cooker) instead of a hot water bath. Although the initial preparation of the jars and food is similar to that of the hot water bath method, the actual process of using the pressure canner is different; so, should you choose this method for your canning needs carefully read and follow all the directions that came with your particular canner. Although the new canners are said to be much safer than the old pressure canners and cookers, they can still blow if something in the process is done incorrectly, creating a potentially dangerous situation. The point is, while it may not necessarily be the best starting place for a preserver just starting out, pressure canning is an excellent tool for the careful canner.

|||||||||||||||||||||||||||||||||||||||||||||||||||||||||||||||||||||||||||||||||||||

After all the jars have had their seals tested, they may be lightly washed, dried, and put on the shelf. Do not submerge the jars into water when cleaning.

Some may say that the pressure canning process will produce a safer food than the hot bath method. However, it all comes down to common sense. Regardless of whether your food has been pressure canned or hot bath canned, you will still need to check your food jars continually, up until the time you consume the food. When canning, no matter which method you use, if the jar does not seal, it cannot be safely put on a shelf and needs to be refrigerated and used quickly. Check the jars already on your shelves from earlier harvests. If the lids have popped (as described earlier in the chapter), DO NOT eat the contents. If the jar looks sealed but the lid falls off with just a little push from your finger, throw the contents away. If the jar is sealed but after opening it the food does not look or smell right, throw it away. It does not matter what method you have used to can it, if it doesn't look or smell right, toss it.

No matter what method you choose to do your canning with, remember to keep it all clean, make sure jars are properly sealed and the foods you are canning are of good quality. Not following the steps of canning, or putting foods that are on the verge of spoiling into the jars will not only end up souring your experience, but will also cost you hours of wasted time and food.

Storage

Storing canned foods is easy. Simply set the jars on a shelf in a cool cupboard in the pantry, in the cellar, or even in a crate in a closet. Because the jars are clear, I normally try to store them out of direct sunlight. And again, it cannot be stressed enough: check your lids at least once every month or so. If a lid is popped, throw it out!

Jellies and Jams

Although most people will group jellies and jams into the same category as canning, jellying was actually its own form of food preservation. The process originated sometime in the early Middle East, although the exact dates are unknown. It was then introduced to Europe during the Crusades, as returning crusaders brought back goods from the front. The technique would come much later to the American colonies, particularly New England, where it was used to preserve fruit for the winter.

The terms jelly and jam are used interchangeably by most people much of the time, but there are actually key differences. Jelly is made using a fruit juice, cooked with sugar and pectin; while jam is a crushed fruit or pulp base cooked with sugar or pectin.

There are also other types of fruit preservation that are similar, but their fruit bases differ:

- **Preserves** use a chunky fruit with sugar and pectin.
- **Marmalade** is like a preserve, but the fruit used is always a citrus with sugar and pectin.
- **Conserve** is a preserve, but instead of only one fruit, two, or more may be used in the mix. Conserves are usually also made with nuts.
- **Fruit butter** is a combination of fresh fruit and spices that are cooked together until thick, then blended (with a blender or a submersible blender) until smooth, then cooked to proper consistency/texture. Apple butter is probably the most well know of the fruit butters.

In making jelly and jam, the sugar is actually acting as the preserving agent. It works by binding the water to prevent (harmful) bacteria growth. Pectin acts as the thickening agent.

Pectin is a carbohydrate, and is found naturally in and around the cell walls of plants. It is used as an ingredient in

An assortment of preserves for making jams. Photo by Vidya Crawley under the Creative Commons Attribution License 2.0.

foods that have a high sugar content, most commonly in jelly, jam, and the other "family members." This is due to the fact that, in order to activate and work correctly, the pectin needs citric acid (or similar acid) and a high sugar content.

Pectin is quite easy to find commercially. Most any grocery store will have it, but it can also be introduced naturally through the addition of a high pectin fruit, such as apples. In fact, in early America apple peel was used in place of pectin for preserving jelly and jam.

Jars, labeled and dated for shelf storage. Photo by Emma Wallace under the Creative Commons Attribution License 2.0.

The process of actually preserving the jelly or the jam is the same as any other canning process. The equipment is the same as in canning, some of which are especially useful when making jams and jellies:

Jars, lids, rings, canner, canning basket (if you have one), canning funnel (this can be very helpful with jelly and jam, as spilling while filling jars can create a sticky mess), clean towels, chopstick or skewer, and jar lifter. Although you can still use tongs if you do not have a jar lifter, you should look into purchasing a lifter if it's within your budget to do so. Should you accidentally drop and break a hot jar of jelly or jam, and it spills on you, it will act like hot sugar and will burn your skin. A jar lifter makes pulling the jars out of the water much safer. If you do not have a lifter, but instead have a canning basket, that will work as well. Just lift the entire basket out and let cool. Once your jars are cooled, do not forget to label and date them for the shelf.

As with canning other foods, jars and rings should be sterilized before using. Check for chips and cracks in the glass, and make sure the rims are clean before putting the lid on. This is especially important with jams and jelly, as drips can turn into sugary build ups on the jar rim. Basically, jar preparation is the same as in any other hot water bath canning. But, it is also important that the outside of your filled jelly and jam jars are wiped thoroughly clean, as any sticky, sugary residue could draw ants to your storage area.

Jars should be filled 1 inch from the top and air bubbles released from the sides before putting the lids on and into the hot bath. Once out of the bath, if the lid feels solid, the seal is good.

If you do not want to have to cook your jelly or can it, you can make what is called freezer jam. Freezer jam need not be cooked, and can be stored in the freezer for up to a year. You can even purchase special plastic storage containers for freezer jam that have a twist on top. Unlike glass these containers are non-breakable which can be important for the freezer.

With freezer jam, you simply mix together your fruit, sugar, and pectin, carefully put the mixture into jars, and freeze. No cooking, no hot water baths, and no pressure canning. Although sterilizing the jars and lids is not strictly necessary when using this method, if I am using glass, I will sterilize anyway. If I am using the plastic freezer jars, I will wash in hot soapy water, and rinse well.

For more ideas and recipes involving canning, please see Recipes, pages 98, 100-103, and 105-106.

CHAPTER 5

FREEZING

·······························

Freezing is a food preservation technique that most everyone uses, but which no one ever thinks of as practicing yet another method of preserving. It is without a doubt one of the easiest and most basic of any of the methods of food preservation (with drying being the other). The one major drawback of freezing, however, is the fact that just one long power outage or a malfunction in your freezer can cost you your harvest.

The equipment needed for freezing (besides a freezer), is very simple and basic as well: bags or containers made specifically for freezer use, along with extra plastic wrap. That is about it. You could also use freezer paper, which is a heavy weighted, white, waxed paper specifically made for wrapping food in for the freezer; however, this is optional.

Equipment and Supplies

Before we go into which foods do and do not respond well to freezing, we need to look closer at the necessary packaging supplies for the proper storage preparation. This will in turn help to eliminate freezer burn (which results from foods drying out in the freezer).

You need to make sure that anything you use to bag or otherwise contain food inside your freezer is actually made for freezer use. Otherwise, you will shorten the storage life of the frozen food and could end up with freezer burnt food. The only time this is not an issue is when you vacuum pack foods, or you purchase foods already vacuum packed (many farmers that sell their own beef package their product this way). Vacuum packed food may be put directly into the freezer as is; however, some preservers will choose to put the entire package, unopened, into a freezer bag for a little extra protection.

As stated earlier, you should only use containers and bags that are made for freezer use. It will be easy to tell if your bags are appropriate, as the packaging will usually be labeled "freezer" or "freezer use." Some people may choose to wrap their foods in aluminum foil before bagging and putting into the freezer. However, if you like to thaw your foods out in the microwave, you will be unable to do so until the food is thawed enough so that the foil unwraps from the food easily and without sticking. This is why it's best to wrap either in plastic wrap or even in freezer paper before putting the food in a freezer bag. It allows the item to go directly from freezer to microwave if you so choose.

Now that you have your equipment, let's look at what can be preserved using the freezing method, and what doesn't work.

Do's and Don'ts of Freezing

One of the major things that does not freeze well is lettuce. If you try to freeze most lettuce varieties, you will have nothing but mush when you bring it out to thaw. Fresh parsley, cilantro, oregano, chives, and other leafy herbs will not freeze well either, especially if you plan on using them as a plate garnish, or in some other way that requires greens in full, fresh form. Again, they will come out mushy when thawed. However, if you want to cook with the herbs, where it will become one of the ingredients for the dish, then freezing is an excellent option for preservation.

Bought some cheese at the farmers market? Blocks of cheese may freeze, but when you go to slice it, they may crumble if you try to cut the pieces straight off the block. If you want cheese crumbles for salads, garnishes, and other similar uses, then this should not be a problem. (I actually keep a few cheddar blocks in the freezer purposely for crumbles.) However, if the idea is to slice some nice pieces of cheese for sandwiches, appetizers, or other uses where you will need the actual slices, then it would be advisable to keep the cheese out of the freezer. In saying this, I have found that crumbled and grated cheeses freeze well and suffer no major changes when thawed. If you're not sure how the cheese you purchased will freeze, take a small piece, wrap it, let it freeze for a few weeks, then take it out and cut it to see what happens. Keep a running list of what cheeses do and do not freeze up to your expectations.

Let's now look at some examples of things that do freeze well, along with tips as to how best to prepare them for freezing.

Fruits and Vegetables

With a few notable exceptions, when freezing fruits and vegetables you do not freeze them whole and will need some preparation before bagging for the freezer. The following are specific examples of prep ideas for various fruits and vegetables.

Bell Peppers

Bell peppers, no matter what color they are, are quite simple and straightforward when it comes to freezing. Just cut the pepper in half, from top to bottom. Remove the stems and seeds, and then cut into strips as wide or as narrow as you like. You can also cut the pepper in half around the wide center, remove the stems and seeds, and cut into rings. From this point, you could just place them in freezer bags and store the filled bags in the freezer. However, there is a better way: instead of your pepper slices having to be thawed first so that they can be broken apart, you will be able to just open the bag, pull out what you want, then put the bag back into the freezer. How is this done? Before you bag your peppers for freezing, simply spread them out on a cookie sheet, on a single layer, and place them in the freezer for a few hours. By doing this, each piece will freeze individually. Once the peppers are well frozen, remove the trays from the freezer and put the frozen pepper pieces directly into the freezer bags. Then put the bag of peppers back into the freezer. By allowing the pepper strips or rings to freeze individually first, the peppers will not freeze all lumped together in the freezer bags. It is important to note however, that at no time should the strips be allowed to thaw, except for those you will be using. Once you allow the bag to thaw when you put it back into the freezer the peppers will stick together and freeze into one big lump.

Tomatoes

Tomatoes will need a little more preparation for freezing, and can be frozen in a few different ways: whole, cut, chopped, puréed, crushed, or as a sauce. However you are freezing them, the tomatoes must be peeled first. (Cherry and grape tomatoes can be an exception to this, as they are usually just cut in half and used, skin and all, in various recipes with no further processing.) While you could just peel the tomatoes like an apple, there is an easier way.

Put water into a medium to large sized pot and bring to a boil. Have a bowl or pot of cold water ready as well. Drop a few whole tomatoes into the pot of boiling water, being careful not to splash. When you see the skins begin to split, remove the tomatoes from the boiling water and plunge them into the cold or iced water. When cool enough to handle, simply pull the skins off with your fingers. They should remove very easily, coming off in almost in one piece, with little to no resistance. Be careful that you do not cook the tomatoes. As soon as you see the skin splitting, remove the tomato from the boiling water and place into the cold water. The cold water will stop the cooking process.

Once the skins are removed you can prepare the tomatoes for freezing whichever way you prefer. But unless you only use your tomatoes one way, I would recommend (if you have enough produce) that you select a few ways to freeze your tomatoes. I usually choose sauce, whole, and purée: sauce, because of the time it would take to make a new batch each time I would want some; whole, because I can always chop them up later if needed; and purée, so that I only have to get out the equipment to do the job once. As these are the most common ways tomatoes are used in recipes, I can pretty much have tomatoes in any way that I need them at my fingertips. I should also note that I can tomatoes in the same three ways. Although I do prefer canning tomatoes, if it is a busy season, freezing is less time-consuming and I can get everything done faster than the time it takes to can. (Otherwise the tomatoes could spoil before I can get to them.) Sometimes I may even go back later, thaw them out and then can the tomatoes when I have more time.

Collard Greens

Because they have such thick heavy leaves, collards will freeze quite well in freezer bags. As the leaves are so large, it is best to chop them up before freezing, as well as stripping them off of the main stock. Because I like them made up with either salt pork or pork jowl, I will usually make a batch (ready-to-eat), then freeze the prepared dish in serving size, re-heatable portions. If you are single, you would probably want to bag and freeze single-serving portions. But for a family, you would most likely freeze at least enough for one serving per person per bag.

Broccoli, Beans, and Other Vegetables

When freezing vegetables like cauliflower, green beans, broccoli, carrots (sliced or baby), and other such vegetables, they should first be cut as desired then blanched. Blanching is just a very quick dip into boiling water, then into an ice bath, or very cold water in a pinch, for a quick cool down to end the cooking process. Blanching allows these vegetables to keep their color and flavor when frozen. The vegetables will still be firm as well.

The key to blanching is a quick in and out of the boiling water, then into the ice water to stop the cooking process. As vegetables blanch you will notice the colors brightening, and they will remain bright even when cool.

After the blanching is done and the vegetables are cooled, freeze as desired. You can use the same freezing method explained previously (see "Bell Peppers," page 41), freezing the pieces individually and bagging. If you are freezing in serving-size bags or containers, and will have no need for the ability to just to pull out a few pieces at a time, then you can bag the cooled vegetables and freeze.

Purées and Juices

Although we will discuss purées and juices later in Chapter 7 as another form of preserving, freezing is a good way to store the finished product. Both purées and juices can be poured into containers and frozen; however, if your main use for the purée or juice is as a recipe ingredient, then you can do one of the following:

Measure out how much juice or purée it takes to fill one cube mold in an ice cube tray. (This will tell you how much product one cube equals.) Then fill the rest of the tray. When thoroughly frozen, take cubes out of the tray and put into a freezer bag. Mark on the outside of the bag the measurement that each cube equals. Then, when you need some of the juice or purée for the dish or for cooking, just pull out the number of pre-measured cubes you need and return the unused portion of the bag to the freezer.

If you think that you may want to freeze your juices or purée into slightly larger portions, simply do the following. Decide the measured amount that you want to freeze the product in. Most likely, this will be in ¼, ⅓, or ½ cup measurements. Pour the measured juice or purée into a small, wax-coated paper cup. Freeze the filled cups. When thoroughly frozen, tear off the paper cup (you may have to slightly warm the sides up with your hand, but do not allow thawing). Then put the frozen pieces into a bag. Label with preserve name in the measurement equivalent of the pieces, and then place the bag in the freezer. Again, pull out pieces as you need them and return unused portions to the freezer.

Soups, Stews, and Sauces

Soups, stews, and sauces have a few ways that they can be frozen. All three may be frozen in freezer containers. Just let cool, pour into the container, and freeze. Also, as a space saver, they may be frozen in plastic freezer bags.

The freezer bag method can be quite a space saver if done properly. And they may be frozen in either single- or multi-portion sizes. To freeze, allow the food to cool. Put the desired amount into the freezer bag. Close the bag, pushing as much air out of it as you can while you close it. (A zip top bag works best for this.) Lay the bags flat, letting content spread evenly into the bag. As you fill and flatten each bag, they can be stacked in your freezer, saving you lots of space.

Finally, if you have made a sauce that will only be used as an ingredient for something else, you may again use the ice cube tray or paper cup method described in the previous section.

At this point, it is important to mention that you need to wait for soups and stews (or any hot food for that matter) to thoroughly cool before you place in the freezer. Placing hot food into the cold freezer can throw your freezer temperature off for a short time, which can result in a longer cooling period than expected.

Make Your Own Frozen Dinner

A final use for freezing is that it allows you to create your own frozen dinners from leftovers.

After you've finished your meal, don't throw away your leftovers, and don't bag each of them separately. Instead, using containers that you can safely freeze in, make a plate in each container. Use one portion of each leftover to make a complete meal. Then cover and freeze. The next time that you need a quick meal for work or home, grab a container, and either microwave it; or if it is an oven safe container as well, put it into the oven. A fast, simple, time-saving meal that uses the same freezing techniques you've been practicing. Don't forget that when you make your regular meals, you can always make extra, especially for this purpose.

A freezer full of preserved food. Photo by Serene Vannoy under the Creative Commons Attribution License 2.0.

There's so much more that you can do with freezing. And there are many books and websites that can give you more information on what you should and shouldn't freeze, as well as directions and suggestions. You'll find some in the Resource section of this book (pages 109 –114).

For more ideas and recipes involving freezing, please see Recipes, pages 102 and 107.

CHAPTER 6

DRYING AND
DEHYDRATING

• •

O ne of the oldest forms of food preservation, drying is a relatively easy process. However, if not done properly (i.e. if foods are not properly dried) then spoilage and mold is a certainty with this method. That having been said, drying is not a difficult process to succeed at. So for some things, it is well worth a try. Drying can be done using the sun (if you live in the right area), the oven, the microwave, or the dehydrator.

Dehydration (or drying) is simply removing all of the moisture from a food. There are many things that can be dried; however, just because something can be dried, doesn't mean that it would be of any use to you in dried form. A good example of this is iceberg lettuce. While you could try to dehydrate lettuce odds are it would not do well and would have no real use. Drying can take a little bit of prep time, and

Dehydrated apples and tomatoes on a drying rack. Photo by Kelly Cree under the Crea-tive Commons Attribution License 2.0.

+ 49 +

you only want to dry or dehydrate what you can and will use from your foods that will dry or dehydrate properly.

However, there is so much that can be dried or dehydrated successfully while maintaining their many culinary uses that it will be a much more difficult chore to decide what you do want to dry or dehydrate, than it would be to avoid those foods that you cannot.

Let's look at some of the more popular items that can be dried or dehydrated, either in a slow oven or dehydrator. You can use the sun as well, if you live in the right region of the country.

Vegetables

Many types of vegetables may be dried for later use. Dried produce can be crumbled for a vegetable-type blend to shake onto food, re-hydrated for use in casseroles, or dried in pieces for later use in soups, where the vegetables will rehydrate on their own in the broth. Some common drying candidates in this category are:

Onions

Onion slices will dry well and have a number of uses when dried. Keep and store onions in slices to use in recipes where large pieces are needed. Crush the dried onion into small flakes for use in soups and other recipes. You can also pulverize and create an onion powder, or create an onion salt by adding salt to the onion powder to taste (sea salt is recommended).

Peppers and Pepper Seeds

Any type of **pepper** or **pepper seed** may be successfully dried; however, unless you are saving seeds for planting, you will most likely dry only hot pepper seeds for culinary use, as a hot pepper's heat is in the seeds. Bell peppers may be dried and flaked for use in soups, chilies, and other similar culinary dishes. They may be dehydrated or dried in strips for later re-hydration in pizzas, casseroles, or fajitas.

Red peppers on a drying rack. Photo by graibeard under the Creative Commons Attribution License 2.0.

Hot peppers, such as cayenne, habanera, jalapeno, and others may be dried whole for later use, flaked, or ground. To keep the heat, remember to include the seeds in your ground or flaked peppers.

Tomatoes

If you are lucky enough to live in an area with lots of hot sun and warm weather, you can make sun-dried tomatoes. Otherwise you will need to dry the tomatoes in your oven or in a dehydrator. Don't worry; it is easier than you might think. Simply slice the tomatoes in half vertically (romas are best for this). You may lightly season however you like with a fine salt—preferably sea salt. Arrange the slices on cake racks. Do not allow the slices to touch. Place cake racks directly onto oven racks in an oven that has been preheated to the lowest possible temperature. Drying time will vary, with five hours usually being the minimum. Tomatoes will be done when they are dry to the touch, but still flexible. They should not be brittle. Remove, let cool, and store in bags or jars, or pack in oil and refrigerate.

Should your tomatoes come out brittle, do not throw them

away. If they do not look or taste burnt, simply crush them into pieces and use as a seasoning. Again, store in a bag or jar in a cool, dry place.

Beans

Fresh beans (including green beans) are easy and fun to dry, and can be a good project for kids who are old enough to use a needle and thread. Simply string the beans, still in their pods, onto a heavy thread, just like stringing popcorn. Hang the string of beans in a cool, dry space out of direct sunlight and allow them to dry thoroughly. When dry, store right on the string or in jars. To use, put in stews, casseroles, and soups. These dried beans in the pod are also called leather britches.

Fruits

You can dry fruits in much the same way that you would dry vegetables.

Racks of drying fruit on dehydrating trays. Photo by La.Catholique under the Creative Commons Attribution License 2.0.

Strawberries

Strawberries that are firm and sweet may be dried using the same oven or dehydrator methods as vegetables. The berries may be cut in half and stemmed, or cut into slices about a quarter of an inch thick. Place the berries on cake racks, then place cake rack on an oven rack in a low temperature oven (as low as possible); or, if using a dehydrator, follow the directions that came with your equipment. Drying time will vary with the size of the berry, drying method, and temperature. The berries may be dried until they have no moisture left but are still pliable, or simply dried to a crisp. To store, place dried berries in an airtight container. Note that dried strawberries will lose quality if they are re-hydrated but will retain quality if they are is stored in the freezer

Bananas

Banana chips are a favorite snack of kids and adults alike. Slice the **bananas** into half-inch discs, dip the discs into lemon juice (to keep the banana from turning brown), place onto a cookie sheet, and put into a low temperature oven, again set to the lowest possible temperature. Check and turn pieces as necessary. Chips are done when dried through and crisp. Once again, if using a dehydrator, follow the directions for your particular machine.

Citrus Peel

Yes, you can dry **citrus peel**; in fact, dried citrus peel is an ingredient in a number of recipes, both culinary and craft, so it is worthwhile to keep the left over peels from your oranges and lemons for drying.

There are two ways to dry citrus peel: as a zest, which is basically grated peel and is the most common version asked for in recipes; or in pieces, normally used for potpourri making. Although citrus zest asked for in recipes is usually fresh, dried zest can be used in a pinch, especially if you don't have fresh available.

To dry zest, simply take the very finely grated peel, spread it out onto a single layer on a plate or tray, and let air dry. You could also dry zest on a sheet of waxed paper, but should you find it necessary be to move it during the drying time, it would be difficult. When thoroughly dry, store in a tightly sealed container.

To dry larger pieces or strips of peel, simply lay on a cookie sheet or plate in a single layer and let dry in a warm, dark spot. In a pinch, you can dry citrus peel in an oven or dehydrator; however, you could end up with burn marks on the peels, so air drying is preferable. Drying time depends on the warmth and dryness of the area that the peel has been set in.

As an extra tip, the white pith on the back of a citrus peel can be quite bitter. Before drying the larger pieces of peel, carefully cut off as much of the pith as possible. Removal of most of the pith will also reduce the thickness of the peel allowing faster and easier drying. When grating the fresh peel into zest, be careful to only grate the pigmented part of the peel and not the pith. Otherwise, you could have a bitter zest.

Meats

Meats may be dried as well. We all recognize it as jerky, a favorite snack of many, including me!

Meats can be trickier to dry than fruits and vegetables, so it is best (and safest) to follow specific recipes when making jerky, at least until you know the correct way to make it. Once you know the correct way to dry meats, you can become creative and make your own recipes.

Although we have only touched on drying and dehydrating you can see how easy it really can be. And as an added bonus, it is a preserving method that, after all the prep work is done, allows you to go about doing other things while the food is drying or dehydrating. Plus, when stored properly, dried or dehydrated foods can last a long time, and are great in emergencies as they do not need refrigeration.

Herbs

There are a few ways to preserve **herbs**: freezing, vinegars and oils (both of which preserve the flavor but not the herb), and drying. Although none of these methods are difficult to carry out, the easiest and most foolproof method is drying. There are a few options open to those looking to dry herbs: microwave (or oven), dehydration, and air drying.

Although **microwave** and **oven** drying work and are the fastest method, you will have to continuously monitor the drying process, lest the herbs crisp too much or even burn, despite the low temperatures you'd be using. It is not a method that you can set and forget until the process is done. Added to that, oven drying is not the most energy efficient method of drying, especially if you are only doing one or two small trays.

Using a **dehydrator** is a bit easier, and is the method to pursue if you want to stick with mechanical means of drying. Although you may not have to watch the herbs as much as with the oven or microwave, you still may need to do a little "rearranging" of trays or plants, depending on the machine you are using.

The best and easiest method to dry your herbs is through **air drying**. And as I already mentioned, it is virtually error proof! Air drying involves simply drying the herbs by hanging or laying on a flat surface, and exposing them to the air to dry. Simply lay out on a cake rack or cookie sheet, or tie the herbs together by their stems and allow them to hang in as dust-free an area as you can manage, well out of direct sunlight (as this can affect the color and possible potency of the herbs). If you are drying the herbs on a cake rack or cookie sheet, you may need to periodically turn the herbs over for even drying.

Once the herbs are thoroughly dry, they may be stored whole, crushed, or pulverized. Store away from direct light, in a dark, cool cupboard or pantry area. An extra layer of protection from too much light, if you need to store on a counter top, would be to store in an amber or other dark tinted container. To preserve the best flavor and keep the plant's oils strong, store the dried herbs whole, and crush or grind as needed. The longer an herb sits pre-ground or crushed, the weaker the oils will become, and the lesser the flavor. Dried herbs do have a shelf life. If your herbs have lost their color or scent, replace with new. Herbs can last a year or more depending on how they are kept and stored.

To **grind** or **crush** your dried herbs, a small electric coffee grinder or mortar and pestle work perfectly, with the grinder being the best way to pulverize an herb. However, when using the coffee grinder, make sure that the grinder you use remains designated for herb and spice use only, as the plastic cover will absorb the oils from the herbs (or spices) and can affect the flavor of your coffee if you grind your beans in it as well.

When hang drying herbs that have seeds (such as dill) that you are planning to keep, before you hang the plant by the stems, put a small, brown lunch bag over the flower heads and lightly tie. Then hang the bunch as usual. The bag will still allow the plant to dry properly, while also keeping the seeds contained as they drop off. When dry, before removing the flower heads from the bag, shake the herb to release any other loose seeds into the bag, then remove the bag (with the seeds) and store the dried herb as you choose. The seeds can be stored for later use.

The **air drying** method is the slowest of all the available methods, but it is a pretty much "set it and forget it" method, especially if you are hanging the herbs.

You can hang dry flowers for craft use as well. This can also be done for edible flowers, to an extent, if you plan to just mix the petals into salads, rubs, or other recipes. However, there is another way to dry flowers if you are using them for craft work only, and that is by using Borax. Using a shoe box, place about two inches of Borax powder in the bottom. Take flower heads (which have been removed from their stem, except for at least one to one and a half inches), and place upside down on top of the powder.

Make sure that the petals are laying properly. Then, gently pour more Borax over the flower heads until they are totally buried including the stub of the stem. From here, drying time can take a few weeks or more. To check your flowers, carefully remove from the powder. If they are dry, they are done. If not, carefully repeat the submersion process and leave them in longer.

You will notice that this process will preserve the flower head in the proper shape and will also do a good job of preserving the color. To "replace" the stem, carefully attach a length (of your choice) of thin floral wire to the stem stub that you left, using floral tape, and use as you like! Remember: this process is for craft use only and NOT for any plants that you will be eating.

CHAPTER 7

PICKLING AND VINEGARS
·····················

It may seem odd to combine pickling and vinegars into one chapter, but the two processes work very well together and play off of one another. Sometimes you may pickle something in straight vinegar and then be able to use the vinegar after preserving is complete; you can make specific vinegars which preserve flavors. Although pickling and vinegars do cross paths many times we'll look at each one separately.

Pickling

What is the first (and for some, the only) thing that pops into mind when the word "pickling" comes up? Pickles, of course; dill pickles, sweet pickles, bread-and-butter pickles; especially in the US, pickling is almost synonymous with pickling cucumbers. But there is much more to pickling and pickles than cucumbers in a pickling solution (brine). When pickling you can create relishes, sauerkraut, fruit, cauliflower, okra, onions, carrots, figs...the list goes on and on. Even eggs and meats can be pickled. As you will see, some pickling doesn't even involve vinegar.

Pickling came about as an answer to the need to preserve foods when there was no refrigeration. Pickles go back as far as 2400 B.C, where it was in use by Mesopotamians. During the Roman Empire, the emperors believed that pickles strengthened a person both spiritually and physically. By 1606, pickles were being produced at home and as a business. Today, pickles are in almost everyone's refrigerator, and we pickle much more than just cucumbers. And nowadays, we pickle because we want to not because we have to.

But how does the most common way of pickling (pickling with vinegar) work? The process basically swaps out the water in a food with vinegar. By soaking the food of choice in a brine first (basically, a saltwater solution), the water is removed from the food. After removal from the brine, the food is then put into a vinegar-based pickling liquid, which will now be allowed to soak into the food. The vinegar will then slow any bacteria growth, which is another preserving property.

There are many different recipes for pickling almost any type of vegetable, and even some fruits. The pickling solutions can be dill, sweet, sour, hot, spicy, or a combination. Once you have made enough pickles from existing recipes, to the point where you are comfortable with the process, you can begin to create your own concoctions for the pickle jar.

Pickling Preparations

So you've decided that you want to do some pickling, but don't know what equipment and supplies will be necessary.

The following is a list of the equipment and supplies usually needed for the process:

- Crock, bowl, or non-reactive pot large enough to hold vegetables for brining
- Strainer and cheesecloth
- Non-reactive pot to cook vegetables in the pickling solution (when called for; not all recipes may call for cooking in the solution)
- Canner, canning jars, lids, and rings

You will also need various spices, salt, herbs, and/or sugars depending on your recipe, as well as vinegar, with white vinegar being the most common type called for.

Also notice that crocks may be used for brining. Yes, crocks are still available for purchase; they can even still be purchased new, although you can use vintage or antique crocks so long as they can still hold liquid. If you have an old crock and are not sure if it will still hold liquid, before you begin to brine in it, place the crock in the tub or shower, fill with water and let it sit for at least 24 hours. If there is no water escaping from any cracks, then the crock should still be fit to use. Empty and clean the crock well. Before adding the brine and food, move the crock to the spot you want it to set. A cool spot is best. Then add brine and food, in no particular order.

Pickling vegetables in vinegar. Photo by Eunice under the Creative Commons Attribution License 2.0.

Don't forget the rules of safe food handling. Your vegetables or fruits n eed to be blemish-free, washed, and fresh. If there are any signs of rot or softness do not use that fruit or vegetable for pickling.

You will also need to prep and sterilize your jars, lids, and rings. From there, follow the directions of the pickling recipe that you have chosen. If you are making a lot of jars of pickles, you will probably choose to proceed with the canning process. However, if you're only making two or three jars of pickles, you may then choose to simply refrigerate the jars instead of using the canning process. Should you choose to simply refrigerate a few jars of pickles, this is fine to do. However, remember that the jars of pickles will not be shelf stable, and will need to remain in the refrigerator, as would any jar you have opened for use.

There is one drawback to pickling. It can increase the salt content of the food, while reducing the vitamins. So if you have a problem with sodium this is something to keep in mind while eating pickled foods.

Pickling with Alcohol

You can also pickle without vinegar. This is done by using alcohol (the drinking kind) as the preserving agent instead of using vinegar. Although not usually a method used for vegetables, although it is possible, preserving fruit in alcohol is a very common practice, especially for holiday use and gifts. And, because it is considered such an easy way to preserve foods, the alcohol method is looked at as almost foolproof, even for the first time preserver. As such, it is a great project for the beginner.

Perhaps you have heard a grandparent, parent, or friend talk about "boozy fruit." This is the result of using alcohol preservation to keep fruit longer. Basically, the fruit is preserved in a mix of alcohol and sugar. The alcohol could be rum, brandy, or a variety of other types of alcohol. The type used, and the ratio of alcohol to sugar will vary with the recipe, as well as the type of fruit used. However, it can also be as simple as putting fruit in a jar, covering the fruit with alcohol, tightly covering, and storing the jar in a cool dark place.

As the alcohol kills bacteria, fruits preserved in alcohol usually will not need refrigeration. However, if you feel better doing so, there is no harm in refrigerating the fruit.

Once the pickled fruit is ready (the amount of time necessary will vary by the recipe, with the length of pickling time being anywhere from a few days to almost a year) what will you do with it? The fruit may be served on ice cream, added to recipes, puréed for use in sauces, dropped into drinks, or used in any other way that works for you. Just remember that you have not cooked the fruit in the alcohol, so the alcohol will still be in the liquid and the fruit. So it is worth keeping this in mind when serving.

Pickling can be a fun preservation project. There are thousands of recipes in books, online, and passed down among the generations for pickling everything from cucumbers to pigs' feet. And once you are comfortable with all of the basics, you can begin to create your own combinations and recipes.

Vinegars

Sometimes pickling can be as simple as putting something in a jar of (usually) white vinegar, in which case not only do you have the pickled food to eat, but the flavored vinegar to use as well. The vinegar will pick up the flavor of whatever you are pickling in it.

Herbs and hot peppers work best for vinegars, as the flavors will release quite nicely, giving you an excellent condiment. Although typically you pickle herbs in vinegar mainly to preserve the flavor of the herb in the liquid, you can use the pickled peppers that you make, as well as the flavored vinegar that will result. The peppers may be put in the vinegar whole, in slices, or in a combination. You can also drop pepper seeds loosely into the vinegar as well, to increase the heat. And don't be afraid to create combinations of peppers and herbs or spices in the same jar. You really cannot make a mistake.

To make this even easier, going through the canning process is not necessary (but sterilizing the jars or bottles you use absolutely is), and all you need to do is let the jars set until you reach the desired flavor. This usually takes at least a few weeks. However, as long as the peppers are in the vinegar, the vinegar will become more potent. If you like the flavor at a certain point, you can remove the peppers from the vinegar, bag, and refrigerate the peppers for later use; the flavor of the vinegar will remain stable. The same holds true for the peppers. And there is no reason that you cannot chop up the pickled herbs and use them in a dish, should you want to try it.

So there you have it: a brief look at the simplicity of pickling. As you can see, it really is more than just a cucumber in a jar. Because there are so many options, you can stay as simple or become as creative as you choose. It is a tasty way to preserve some of your garden leftovers for later.

For more ideas and recipes involving pickling, please see Recipes, pages 99 and 104.

CHAPTER 8

CURING AND SMOKING

• •

uring, a method used to preserve meats and fish, can be used as a preservation method on its own or as a prelude to the smoking process. It is a method of preservation using salt, sugar, and/or nitrate, with salt being the key ingredient in the curing process, while sugar and nitrate may be optional. No matter what method you choose, salt is always part of the curing process.

Curing

Salt removes water from the meat, slowing its oxidation and preventing the meat from becoming rancid. And, although the salt by itself does not actually kill the bacteria it does slow it down.

Sugar plays against the strong flavor of the salt and feeds beneficial bacteria. During the curing process, sugar may take the form of maple syrup, corn syrup, white or brown sugar, or honey.

Nitrates kill harmful bacteria, enhance flavor, and provide the appealing red or pink color that cured meats have. Without nitrates the meat takes on an unappetizing gray color. However, while nitrates are a necessary ingredient in curing sausage (and other dry meats) to prevent botulinum toxin (which causes botulism) the use of nitrates is now in question. This is due to the fact that when there is a high concentration of nitrates present, and the cured food is cooked at high temperatures, nitrosamines may be produced which may be carcinogenic in animals. While the debate goes on, some find celery juice to be a respectable replacement for nitrates. But like nitrates, this too is under debate as to whether it is a good replacement or not. In the end, it comes down to the individual doing their due diligence and choosing their preferred method.

Methods of Curing

There are four methods of curing:

- Dry
- Wet
- Combination
- Salt curing

Dry Curing

Dry curing is a salt cure with nitrates. A rub mixture is applied generously by hand. The meats are then packed tightly into a tub or large container, with drainage. Curing time will depend on how much meat is being cured, but the rule of thumb is two days per pound for small cuts of meat and three days per pound for larger cuts, such as ham and pork shoulder. Dry cured meats will experience a 15–20 percent loss in water weight.

Dry curing is the best method to use in hot climates. It is excellent for curing bacon, ham and sausages, especially if you plan on air drying.

Wet Curing

Wet curing is basically curing using a salt water base, also known as a brine. The addition of sugar turns it into a sweet brine, which some may also refer to as a sweet pickling brine.

Wet curing is commonly used with hams or butts and is most

often used in conjunction with smoking. It is a slow method, with the meat being submerged into the brine for up to two weeks at 40 degrees.

This curing process also has some other drawbacks. The meat will need to be turned for even distribution of the solution. The surface of the brine solution will need to be skimmed periodically to prevent possible contamination.

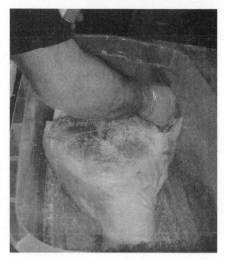

Curing prosciutto in a sea salt solution. Photo courtesy of Wikimedia Commons.

There is also a risk of the meat spoiling, especially close to the bone, if not done correctly. Therefore, if this is your method of choice, spend some time doing your homework on the proper way to wet cure the cut of meat that you have selected.

Combination

The **combination** method of curing is simply using a combination of the dry and wet curing methods. In using this method, the dry cure is done first then after a few days brine is added to the container, immersing the meat. (For the combination method, you do not want to use a container with drainage). Curing time will depend on the cut of meat, but can range from four days on up, after which the meat would be smoked, usually using the cold smoked method (see "The Methods of Smoking"on page 71).

Salt Curing

Basically another form of dry curing, **salt curing** is still used with some meats. The difference between this and dry curing is the absence of nitrates in the salt rub. Air-dried hams, such as prosciutto, are cured in this way.

The salt concentration needs to be at least 10 percent for safety purposes. Salt curing is the fastest method of curing, as it quickly pulls and removes the water from the meat. Curing time with this method will depend on the meat, but an average 10 pound ham could take up to seven months to complete, as salt curing also involves air drying the meat and not smoking it.

It should be noted that along with the salt, nitrate, and/or sugars, herbs and spices may be added to the curing rubs or brine for additional flavor.

Smoking

One method of preservation that has been making a big comeback in home preserving is **smoking**. Once common only on farms, where the family smokehouse would preserve meats so that after the late fall/winter slaughter time the family could be kept in meat through the winter, today smokers and small smokehouses can be found in many backyards, small camps, and restaurants throughout the country.

The smoking of foods is done slowly using low heat. You can smoke meats, cheese, fish, peppers (chipotle peppers are simply smoked jalapeños), and more.

The Types of Smoking

There are four types of smokers that are normally used by the home smoker:

- Electric
- Charcoal
- Propane
- Water and steam

The first three options—electric, charcoal, and propane—are the most common types found in the home. However, if a smoker is not an option for you at this point, then a regular charcoal grill can also work by putting heat on one side only while the meat sits on the cold side. This will give the same indirect heat and smoke result that you would get from a small backyard smoker.

As smokers come in all different sizes, shapes and types, you will need to operate yours according to the specific instructions that come with it. And, at least for the first few times that you use it, it would also be advantageous to use the recipes that either came with the smoker or are in a cookbook

Meat smoking in an open smoker. Photo by Cookipediachef under the Creative Commons Attribution License 2.0.

with recipes specifically for smokers. Once you have the know-how you can go off on your own and create some of your own dishes. But, there is one point of instruction which is necessary to follow with all smokers. When you are filling your smoker with the food you are planning to smoke do so only in the amounts recommended by the manufacturer. Otherwise it can slow down the smoking process. In addition, the food should not touch each other, as this can lead to underdone spots on your food, especially if you started with raw meats.

The Methods of Smoking

Along with there being different types of smokers, there are also different methods of smoking. The two methods or processes that the home smoker will commonly use are:

- Hot smoking
- Cold smoking

The **hot smoking method** is what typically comes to mind when a person thinks of smoking food. This method uses both smoke and heat, fully cooking the foods that are (usually) hung in the smoker. Because this method fully cooks the foods and kills most of the common bacteria, you can usually eat hot smoked foods without any additional cooking. Hot smoking is what gives you the pink smoke ring on meats (which you would see when cutting the meat open), under the bark (or crust) or skin. The short, very simple explanation of a smoke ring is that it is caused by a reaction of gases from the smoke and the myoglobin (the pigment which gives muscles their color) in the meat. It is worth mentioning that while these pink smoke rings are coveted among smoked meat enthusiasts, it does not seem to add to the flavor of the meat.

Hot smoking temperature is at least 150°F.

Cold smoking is for flavor enhancement only. The meat must be already cured beforehand, as cold smoking does not cook the meat. It is basically smoking without the heat.

Cold smoking temperature is usually at 100°F or less.

Hanging meat preserving in a smokehouse.

Flavorful Fuels

When using smokers—especially charcoal, but with the other types of smokers as well—wood is needed to create the smoke that will preserve and flavor the meat. Due to their slow burning traits and lack of sap or resin, hardwoods are commonly used. The most popular types are apple, mesquite, oak, hickory, maple, cherry, and pecan. It used to be that the type of wood you used depended upon what was readily available in your area. Now, with the availability of all types of hardwood chips and chunks for smoking in any number of home, hardware, and outdoor stores the available choices are much less limited.

The process of producing the smoke simply consists of wet wood chips or chunks interacting with a heating source within the smoker, with the source dependent upon the type of smoker being used. The smoke and heat both cures (basically cooks) and preserves the food.

Brining

Some foods (primarily meats) will need some preparation before being placed within the smoker. This is so that the meat does not dry out during the smoking process. This process is called brining. Brine is basically a saltwater solution that will add approximately 10 percent water weight to the meat, which will help to offset the 20 percent water weight that the meat will lose during the smoking process. The percentage of saltwater will depend on the meat being smoked. Any brining recipe you use will give you the correct percentage, but it is usually a 3 percent solution (2 tablespoons salt per 1 quart water) or a 6 percent solution (4 tablespoons salt per 1 quart water). Many brine recipes will also add a sweetener such as sugar or honey, to prevent the smoked meat from becoming too salty. Brining can take anywhere from hours to days depending on the recipe. When the meat is removed from the brine the brine should be discarded, as it will now contain raw meat juices and is not safe to reuse.

A chicken brining in a cooler. Photo by Andrew Malone under the Creative Commons Attribution License 2.0.

Once the meat is removed from the brine, it can be put into the smoker as is; additionally, it can be given an extra layer of flavor by using a dry rub or marinade before smoking. This is only an option. The average smoking time of meat is one and a half hours per pound; however, this may vary based on your smoker's performance or the meat you are using. As with any meat, smoked meat should be at the correct temperature for that particular meat before removing from the smoker. Always test the smoked meat with a meat thermometer before removing. Some recipes may call for the meat to be "fall off the bone" done. This is just as it says – the meat will actually fall right off the bone when ready. Smoked meat should also be moist and tender.

When smoking cheese, cold smoking is the process that is used; you want to flavor the cheese, not cook it. There is no set time to cold smoke your cheese; continue smoking until you get the color and flavor that you're looking for.

Vegetables can be easily smoked by cutting them into chunks or pieces (depending on the vegetables you are using), placing them in a pan, brushing them with oil and putting them in a smoker until tender. Some, like peppers, may be smoked whole.

Smoking will give foods a wonderful flavor, but it is also a slow process that will take time and patience. It will also take time to master. You will need to watch your temperatures, making sure the smoker maintains the necessary heat level for what you are doing, and adjust the smoker accordingly as per its directions when necessary. Although it is not a process where you can preserve your food and have it ready to eat in a half hour, and it is not an instant gratification way of preparing food, the finished product is definitely worth the wait.

CHAPTER 9

ADDITIONAL METHODS OF PRESERVING

Along with the preserving methods discussed in the preceding chapters, there are also a few more methods of preservation that warrant a quick mention. These methods are:

- Root cellars
- Vacuum packing
- Oil
- Purée and Juices

Let's take a quick tour of each of these methods.

Root Cellars

Root cellars are used to keep foods at a low temperature, while keeping the humidity at an even level. Because they are underground, root cellars will prevent food from freezing in the winter and keep them cool during the summer.

A root cellar built into a hillside. Illustration by Ariel Delacroix Dax.

Usual foods stored in root cellars include potatoes, parsnips, turnips, onions, apples, cabbage, squash, and the like. Root cellars may be separate buildings or a part of the home cellar, as long as it is not heated. (So if your furnace is in your cellar, your cellar will be too warm to be a root cellar.)

When storing food in a root cellar, there are foods that should not be stored together. Fruit such as apples and pears contain a gas called ethylene that can hurt the flavors of root foods such as potatoes if kept in close proximity.

Root vegetables in a root cellar. Illustration by Ariel Delacroix Dax.

However, problems such as this can be avoided. If your root cellar is large enough, you can create a second room to store the ethylene-containing foods separately from the rest. If you have high shelves, you can also store those particular foods on the tops of the shelves. There are a number of options for storage, including creating a second cellar. The best thing that you can do if you're considering a root cellar is to do your homework. Figure out what is best for your needs, the space that you have available and what your budget can handle; then make your decision. You might also check to see if you will need any permits.

As the root cellar has been making a comeback in the last few years, there are many sites and plans for them online, as well as in books and magazines. I have included some examples of these in the Resource section at the end of this book (see pages 109-114).

Vacuum Packing

Once available almost exclusively on a commercial basis, vacuum packing has been available for the home food preservationist for a number of years, and has become quite popular within the last 10 to 15 years or so. Although vacuum packaging in bags is most widely used, containers for vacuum packaging are also available for home use.

Vacuum packaging involves simply removing all of the air from your package, which inhibits—but not necessarily eliminates—bacterial growth and lengthens the shelf life of the food. This method may be used for both frozen foods and dry foods.

Although vacuum packaging is a good way to extend shelf life and save storage space, as well as being relatively easy to do if you have the equipment, home vacuum packaging is not a replacement for refrigeration or freezing. You will still need to refrigerate or freeze your preserves.

But if you lack space, vacuum packaging may be an option to further explore.

Oil

When preserving with oil, you are basically preserving the flavor of the food that you have packaged in it not the food itself. This method is also known as infusing oils. Olive oil is the best oil to use, however canola oil will also work well. It should be noted that olive oil will tend to go rancid.

You should only use good quality herb leaves, garlic, spices, or peppers. The herbs may be fresh or dry, and spices may be whole or ground, but the ground spices (or herbs) need to be wrapped in cheesecloth before submerging into the oil. This will make it easier to pull the little pieces of herbs or spices out of the oil.

Although there are a wide range of recipes available for oil infusions, there are basically two ways to prepare them: cold infusion and hot infusion.

Cold infusion involves simply taking your flavoring ingredients, dropping them into a bottle or jar of warm oil, and then sealing and letting it sit for at least two weeks, to allow the flavor to infuse into the oil.

Hot infusion, by contrast, involves heating the oil and ingredients together in a sauce pan, a heavy bottom pan is best, until you can actually smell the flavor in the oil. Bottle or jar it, allow to cool, refrigerate, and use within a few weeks. Heat infused oil allows for immediate use, as cold infused requires waiting for the flavors to meld with the oil.

Infused oil is fun to make, and if doing a cold infusion, the kids can even help. When you are ready there are hundreds of recipes online, in books and magazines available to start you off. Just like with the vinegars, once you become proficient and comfortable with the process you can create your own recipes as well!

Purée and Juice

When you think about purées and juices you don't normally think about these two foods being former preserves. However, they are considered as such. A purée is a fruit or vegetable that has been cooked and strained or has been processed in a blender or food

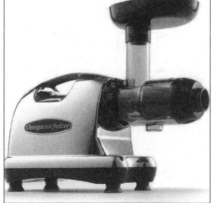

A ceramic depression juicer.   An electric juicer.

processor, while juice is the liquid that has been extracted or squeezed from a fruit or vegetable, usually with some type of juicer or juice extractor. Both can be quite simple to make.

Purées are much thinner than a jam or a jelly but thicker than a

Using a juicer to make wheatgrass juice. Illustration by Ariel Delacroix Dax.

juice. It is a pure fruit composition, containing no extra sugars or pectin. Purées are also used mainly as a sauce or as an ingredient for a recipe, while juice is for drinking as well as for cooking. With a purée, you are preserving the fruit, albeit in a prepared form instead of whole or chunked. With juice, you are preserving the flavor of the fruit or vegetable, and not the fruit or vegetable itself.

Both purées and juices may be frozen, canned, or refrigerated. Most any fruit or vegetable can be puréed or juiced, and most households will already have the equipment in their kitchens to make these foods.

There are many recipes for both purée and juices, again in books, online, and in magazines. And as with many other methods, once you are familiar with the process of puréeing and/or juice making, you can create your own tasty concoctions. Freezing fresh purée or juice in molds or in paper cups (with sticks inserted in the center) makes delicious popsicles, without all the extra sugar and colorings. Just a suggestion!

Making your own purées and juices is just one more way that you can preserve foods. Both processes are fairly easy to do, with minimal steps involved, and can be a great option for those who are looking for alternative preserving methods.

CHAPTER 10

WHEN PRESERVED FOODS GO BAD

f course, food preservation is not perfect; even with the most careful preparations preserved foods can still go bad.

Dried or Dehydrated Foods

Dried foods, if exposed to any type of moisture, can mold. With foods that have been completely dried or dehydrated, moisture has been completely removed, preventing the food (for the most part) from spoiling. However, if just a little moisture is in some way introduced into the bag or container that the dry food is being stored in the once dried food can now mold if not refrigerated and used quickly. Even so little as a few drops of any type of moisture can ruin an entire bag or container of dried foods, if it is not caught in time. If you believe moisture has been introduced into your stock of dried food, either refrigerate the food; or, if it is an item that freezes well, you can freeze the dried food.

Canned Food

As discussed in Chapter 4, if the lid pops on a jar of canned food the contents must be discarded; the food has lost the seal which had acted like a vacuum and protected the contents.

But why would a jar, if it was firmly sealed when it went onto the shelf, all of a sudden have a popped lid? This could be a result of a few things. There could have been a small chip in the rim of the jar, tiny enough to allow initial sealing but big enough to prevent the seal from staying intact for long. Sometimes you can get faulty lids, and unfortunately you will not know whether this is the case until it is too late. Another possibility is that you may not have left the jars in the hot water bath long enough to create the seal. There can be many reasons for lids popping, but these are a few of the most common.

Frozen Foods

Frozen foods go bad in two main ways. First is **freezer burn**, which is when the foods actually dry out in the freezer. This can happen if the food has been in the freezer for too long, or if the food has not been packaged correctly, such as not using bags or containers suitable for freezing. Putting meats in the freezer in the packages they came in (plastic wrap and foam tray) or not properly resealing an open bag before returning it to the freezer can also run you the risk of freezer burn.

The second way that frozen food can go bad in the freezer is due to a **power failure**. Now, this may seem like a rather obvious problem; however, you can help to stave off the loss of foods by doing just a few things. Don't keep opening the freezer or leave the freezer door standing open. The less you go into your freezer during a power outage the more cold air remains inside. If the shelf is packed tight, try to leave it alone during the outage if possible. Tight packaging of frozen foods will keep the foods frozen longer.

If you have a winter outage, with temperatures outdoors that are consistently below freezing, and if you have frozen food in the freezer, pack it up and move it outside into a garage or shed where it will stay cold and out of the reach of animals. If it is cold enough, the food may even remain frozen. (This option should only be considered if you have food thawing, and are at risk of losing the food, with outdoor temperatures that are extremely cold/below freezing.)

Oils and Vinegars

Infused oils, like any other oil, may go **rancid**, which you will be able to identify by its having a different smell or appearance than it should. Any time your infused oil doesn't look or smell right discard it. I have never had vinegar go bad.

Cured and Smoked

Cured or smoked foods can go bad if the process is not done properly or if the end results are not stored correctly.

These are only a few examples of preserved foods going bad. Sometimes this can be prevented through common-sense handling. Other times there is little you can do to prevent spoilage, as it can be dependent on conditions outside of your control. That is all a part of preserving foods. But, the more you do it the more you learn about the process and the better able you are to lessen your losses during an emergency.

Remember, when you have losses or spoilage it may be a bit disheartening. But as I said, it does come with the territory. Don't let it stop your enthusiasm!

FINAL NOTES

The act of preserving one's harvest goes back thousands of years. In those days, it was a way to have food throughout the winter, when crops or gardens could not be grown, or when meat had to be stored after the winter slaughter, or after the periodic hunting excursions. For those periods in the historic timeline when refrigeration and freezers didn't exist, although they were imperfect, their methods worked pretty well. So well, in fact, that even with the refrigeration and freezing technology that we have today we still use these same methods of food preservation.

While some of the methods in this book may take a little time to get the hang of, none are impossible to learn, and with a little practice anyone can become proficient. By using many of these preservation methods, even those households without a freezer can safely store food for later use.

The chapters in this book give the new food preservationist a good introduction to the various methods of food preservation. From here, you decide which method or methods you want to use. It is recommended that you do a little further study and familiarize yourself on the different choices available to you. When additional equipment is involved, always read any and all instructions that came with it before you begin. And, if you know someone who already uses one of these methods, the next time they are working on preserving, ask to help. Not only will it be the best way to learn a new skill, it's a good excuse to get together with a friend on a Saturday!

Here's to your success in harvest preservation.

Enjoy!

HELPFUL HINTS

When using the boiling water method to peel a large quantity of tomatoes, the cold bath water will need to be changed periodically, as it will begin to heat up from the warm fruit. As you change the water, put the "used" liquid aside in another vessel. This will come in handy when you are either packing your tomatoes into jars or making sauce and find that you need to add additional liquid (which would usually be plain water).

Using the tomato water rather than plain water, allows you to add additional liquid while minimizing loss of flavor. When you are done packing or making your sauces, discard the leftover water. (You can always add it to the compost pile if you have one.)

When freezing strawberries whole, remove the stem/hull area before packaging. As berries will not be as firm after thawing, hulling will be a bit messier if you wait. The other advantage is that the berries will be ready to use, however you choose, as soon as they are thawed.

When substituting dried herbs for fresh, keep in mind that dried herbs are stronger than the fresh. This is due to the higher concentration of the oils through the drying process. As a result, although you can substitute one for the other, the ratios will change. The substitution ratio is 3:1 (or ⅓ dried = 1 part fresh). So whatever your recipe calls for in fresh herbs, use ⅓ of the amount in dried. If substituting fresh for dry, then just flip the ratio (for example, if the recipe for ⅓ teaspoon of dried herb, substitute 1 teaspoon fresh).

When curing, always follow the recipe precisely, at least until you are 100 percent comfortable in creating your own cures. If done wrong, you could end up with tainted or spoiled meat.

Periodically, rearrange your freezer and the cupboard or pantry that you keep your canned foods in. Check the dates on your packages, and put those with the earliest dates in the front, to be used first. When restocking the freezer or pantry with like foods (for example, adding new containers or jars of soups to the soup shelf), the new jars or packages should be placed behind the older ones. Again, this allows you to use the foods that have been in the longest, first.

If you have some canning jars with a tiny chip in the rim (no cracks), but you feel like you are "wasting" the jars by throwing them into recycling because the chip is so tiny you can't see it, they can be safely re-purposed. Even though they are not safe to can with, the jars may still be used to store candy, dried herbs, sugar, buttons, even seed packs. However, if the chip is large, rough or sharp or there is any sign of cracking, under no circumstance should you use the jar in any way. And remember, even a jar with a tiny chip in the rim can crack once it hits hot dish water!

RECIPES

. . . .

Homemade Stocks

One thing that you will discover as you begin homesteading is that there is a use for everything, no matter how small it is. If done properly, few things will go to waste on the homestead. One of the best examples of this is in making stock for soups and other needs. You can make chicken, beef, pork, ham, turkey, and vegetable stock from the recipes below.

Once created, each of these stocks may be turned into soups or used as bases for other recipes. To turn any of these stocks into soup, simply add your choice of shredded or chunked meat and/ or sliced or chunked vegetables or potatoes, and cook slowly until meat is cooked and vegetables are tender. You can make your soup with as thin or as thick with meat and/or vegetables as your family likes.

Chicken Stock

When you've finished preparing that roast chicken, hang on to the carcass and freeze it until you're ready to make your stock. Also, when chicken thighs go on sale at the store (or if you raise chickens for meat yourself) buy a bag. While you can use a whole chicken, thighs are less expensive and are flavorful.

Put the chicken carcass and chicken into a large stock pot. Cover with water until the chicken and carcass are just covered, up to a couple inches over. Let simmer on a medium-low to medium heat, checking frequently and adding more water as it evaporates. DO NOT let the water get low. As soon as the chicken is exposed add more water. Continue to simmer and add water until the stock is ready. The amount of time required will vary greatly, but when you try to pull out a piece of chicken and it just falls apart, your stock is ready.

At this point, you can either just remove the bones and any gristle remaining; or, if you want only stock, remove the meat as well. Do not throw the meat away, as the meat will work well for chicken salad, chicken and biscuits, or other recipes calling for chicken chunks.

Let the broth sit and cool. As it cools, the fat will float to the top. Although you will want to skim a lot of this off, leaving some in the broth will add to the flavor. The amount you leave in will depend on your own taste. Once the fat is removed, you can also season the broth with salt and pepper to taste, or leave plain and season as you use.

This broth may be made into soup right away or may be canned or frozen for future use.

Vegetable Stock

Vegetable stock is made in very much the same way as chicken stock. In fact, all stocks are created in basically the same way with just the base ingredient changing.

Most any vegetable mix may be used for stock, but celery is usually a staple, as it gives flavor. From there, carrots, onions, greens, turnips, almost anything can be added to the mix. (Beets are among the few that are not commonly used.) Cover the vegetables in the same way as was done with the chicken and follow the same procedures. When the vegetables are soft, the stock is done.

You can strain and discard the vegetables (again, composting would be a good use); or, if you like, you may chop up some of the vegetables and return them to the stock. Some will even purée some of the cooked vegetables into the stock, creating a thicker puréed stock.

Store in the same way as chicken stock.

Turkey Stock

Follow the same instructions as for chicken stock. Many times a large, leftover carcass will be enough, but if not, throw in some wings, legs, or whatever you like.

Beef or Pork Stock

Follow the same procedures as the other stocks. Beef or pork bones may be purchased in the store or from butchers. If you know someone who is slaughtering, you may be able to get "soup bones" from them.

Ham Stock

Substitute ham bones. Depending on the size of the bones and the amount of meat still remaining, you may need a few. Follow the same procedure as with previous stocks.

For a richer, darker stock, roast any bones or vegetables in the oven first, then make your stock using the roasted bones or vegetables. It will give your stock a very different flavor and is delicious!

Melon Vodka

6 cups melon (of your choice)

2 ½ cups vodka

Cube the melon and place in a large jar that has a lid. Pour the vodka over the top, pushing the melon down to be sure that it is thoroughly covered with the liquid. Cover and let sit five to seven days.

Strain the melon from the liquid, pressing the melon in the strainer so that all the liquid is extracted. Discard the remains of the fruit and pour the liquid back into a covered jar. Refrigerate.

Sweet Pickling Brine

Brine

4 cups vinegar (apple cider preferred, but white vinegar is acceptable)

8 cups white sugar

2 tablespoons pickling spice

2 tablespoons whole cloves

Pickles

An assortment of vegetables and hot peppers such as cauliflower florets, pearl onions, Jalapeno or other hot pepper.

8-10 pint jars and lids

8-10 small cinnamon sticks (optional)

Extra pickling spice (optional)

Place pickling spice and cloves in the center of a square of cheesecloth, gather, and tie into a bundle. Place sugar, vinegar, and spice packet into non-reactive pot. Cook on medium to medium high heat, stirring, until sugar completely dissolves.

Place an assortment of vegetables and hot peppers into jars. For extra garnish, place a cinnamon stick and ¼ teaspoon pickling spice into jar. For extra spice, slice the peppers and let seeds flow into the jar. For less spice, leave peppers whole. For no spice, eliminate the hot peppers. The jar should be filled one in from the top.

When brine is done, carefully fill each jar with brine. Again it should be no higher than 1 inch from the top. Cover with lid and ring and proceed with the canning process. If you are doing only a couple jars, you can choose to cover and refrigerate.

Green or Yellow Beans

Snip ends of fresh beans and discard. Cut the rest of the beans into halves, thirds or leave whole. Blanche beans quickly, just until they brighten in color (only a couple minutes). Do not cook. Remove and plunge into ice water.

Spoon beans into jars, with quart or pint, depending on your needs, keeping at least one inch from the top of jar. Fill jar with water, using the water you blanched the beans in. Cover and proceed with the canning process. You may add a pin of salt to the jars before covering, if you choose.

To Freeze the Beans

Follow the directions as far as snipping, halving or thirds and blanching. Fill zipper freezer bag one-half to three-quarters full. Close the bag and lay flat. Reopen the bag half way, and slowly and carefully press the air out of the bag as you close. There should be a nice, flat layer of beans in the bag at this time.

Place in freezer, laying flat, stacking subsequent bags on top of the other.

Carrots

Wash carrots. Snip off ends. If the carrot is nice and clean, peeling is optional. When all carrots are prepped, blanche just until color pops. Remove and plunge into ice water.

When cool enough to handle, dice, slice in half, or cut carrot as desired. Fill jars. Using the water you blanched with, fill jars to 1 inch. Cover and proceed with canning process.

To Freeze the Carrots

Follow the directions as far as snipping, halving, chopping, and blanching. Fill zipper freezer bag one half to three fourths full. Close the bag and lay flat. Reopen the bag half way, and slowly and carefully press the air out of the bag as you close. There should be a nice, flat layer of carrots in the bag at this time. Place in freezer, laying flat, stacking subsequent bags on top of the other.

Tomatoes

Peel tomatoes. Remove core. Halve, crush, or leave whole. Fill jar to at least one in from top. Cover and proceed with canning process.

To Freeze Tomatoes

Follow the directions as far as snipping, halving, chopping, and peeling. Fill zipper freezer bag one-half to three-quarters full. Close the bag and lay flat. Reopen the bag half way, and slowly and carefully press the air out of the bag as you close. There should be a nice, flat layer of tomatoes in the bag at this time. Place in freezer, laying flat, stacking subsequent bags on top of the other.

Variations

When canning beans, carrots, tomatoes, or other such foods, you can add flavor to some or all of the jars, simply by adding garlic or garlic powder, Italian seasoning, basil, or other herbs and/or spices to the individual jars, before sealing. (This does not flavor as well when adding to foods you will freeze.)

Peaches in Light Syrup

Syrup

2¼ cups sugar

5¼ cups water

Cook water and sugar in pot (stainless is best) until sugar is completely dissolved, stirring continuously to prevent burning. Makes approximately six cups.

Peaches

Peel peaches, cut in half, and remove pits. Either leave in halves or quarter.

Place fruit in pint or quart jars, leaving at least 1 inch from top. Spoon in syrup over fruit, again leaving 1 inch from top. Cover and proceed with canning process.

Pickled Garlic

2 cups garlic cloves (peeled)

1 cup white sugar

1 teaspoon canning salt

3 cups white vinegar

Blanch garlic cloves for about one minute. Do not allow garlic to cook or soften.

Combine vinegar, sugar, and salt in stainless pan. Bring to boil with sugar completely dissolved.

Pack garlic into prepared canning jars, pint or quart sized. Pour syrup over garlic. Using funnel will make this easier. Leave at least 1 inch from top. Before covering with lid wipe rim clean with damp, lint free cloth. Cover and proceed with canning process.

Garlic Dills

5 pounds cucumbers cut into spears or medallions (pickling type work best but any can be used)

1 teaspoon powdered alum

8 cloves garlic

8 teaspoons dill seed

1 quart white vinegar

2 quarts water

1 cup salt

Wash cucumbers and drain. Slice and pack into prepared quart jars. To each jar, add ¼ alum, two garlic cloves, and two teaspoons dill seed.

Combine vinegar, water, and salt in large stainless pan. Bring to a boil.

Spoon the hot liquid into cucumber filled jars. Leave at least 1 inch from top. Before covering, clean rim with damp, lint free cloth. Cover and proceed with canning process.

Strawberry Preserves

2 quarts fresh strawberries, washed, hulled, and halved

¼ cup lemon, finely chopped and seeded

¼ cup water

1 (1 ¾ ounce) package powdered pectin

7 cups sugar

Combine strawberries, lemon, water, and pectin in large, stainless steel pot. Bring the mixture to a boil, stirring continuously. Add sugar and return mixture to a full, rolling boil. Stir constantly. Continue the boil for one minute. Remove the hot mixture from heat and skim off any foam from top.

Spoon the berry mixture into prepared jars. Remove air bubbles. Wipe rim of jar with damp, lint free cloth before covering. Proceed with canning process, allowing jars to remain in bath approximately 15 minutes.

Freezing Corn on the Cob

Shuck the corn, removing all husks and the silk. Trim ends if needed and remove any bad spots on ear of corn. Blanch.

When cool, individually wrap each ear in plastic wrap, then arrange in freezer bags. Usually three to four ears will fit in a bag. Seal and place flat in freezer.

Note that you may skip the plastic wrap step.

RESOURCES

Websites

National Center for Home Food Preservation (http://nchfp.uga.edu)
Very informative site on home food processing.
(http://nchfp.uga.edu/publications/uga/using_press_canners.html)
Good site for further information on pressure canning

Website of Colonial Williamsburg (www.history.org)
Excellent website for historically based information on Colonial America.

Ball Canning (www.freshpreserving.com)
The Ball canning website, includes information and recipes.

Kansas Historical Society (www.kshs.org)

The New Century Homesteader (www.thenewcenturyhomesteader.blogger.com)
Workshops and programs. Feel free to contact with questions on any aspect of backyard farming.

Food Safety and Preservation, Washington State University, Clark Co. Extension (http://clark.wsu.edu/family/FoodSafetyWebsitesAndPublications2011.pdf)

How Food Preservation Works (http://science.howstuffworks.com/innovation/edible-innovations/food-preservation.htm)

UNL Food: Home Food Preservation, University of Nebraska, Lincoln (http://food.unl.edu/web/preservation/canning)

Organic Gardening Magazine–Rodale: Refrigerator Pickles (www.organicgardening.com/cook/refrigerator-pickles)

Organic Gardening Magazine–Rodale: Building a Root Cellar (www.organicgardening.com/learn-and-grow/building-root-cellar-your-home)

Allrecipes.com (http://allrecipes.com/howto/smoking-foods/)
Short how-to on smoking.

TLC (http://recipes.howstuffworks.com/tools-and-techniques/how-to-smoke-foods.htm)
Short article and video on smoking food.

USDA: Grilling and Smoking Food Safety (http://dwb.unl.edu/teacher/nsf/c10/c10links/www.fsis.usda.gov/oa/pubs/grilsmok.htm)

The Old Farmer's Almanac: Building a Root Cellar (www.almanac.com/root-cellar-build)

University of Missouri Extension: Root Cellar Storage Requirements (http://extension.missouri.edu/p/MP562)

USDA Smokehouse Plans (www.meatsandsausages.com/ smokehouse-plans)

LSU Ag Center: Smokehouse Plans (www.lsuagcenter.com/en/ our_offices/departments/Biological_Ag_Engineering/Features/ Extension/Building_Plans/food/smokehouse/)

Periodicals

Smoked Cheese Bulletin, W.C. Wendorff, Wisconsin Center for Dairy Research, University of Wisconsin.

Countryside Magazine (www.coutrysidemag.com)
One of the first in self-sufficiency. Lots of articles on beekeeping.

Mother Earth News (www.motherearthnews.com)
One of the first magazines for those interested in homesteading and self-sufficiency. A variety of articles about food preservation.

Acres USA: The Voice of EcoAgriculture (www.acresusa.com)
Excellent magazine for sustainable and organic farming. Lots of articles for the small and backyard farmer.

Organic Gardening Magazine (www.organicgardening.com)
Magazine for the organic gardener and small farmer. Covers rural, suburban, and urban all across the country. Includes occasional articles about preserving food.

Books

Farmstand Favorites: The Complete Home Guide to Canning and Preserving, Hatherleigh Press, 2012.

Anderson, Warren R. *Mastering the Craft of Smoking Food.* Short Hills, NJ: Burford Books, 2006.

Bills, Jay, and Shirley Bills. *Dehydrating Food: A Beginner's Guide.* New York: Skyhorse Pub., 2010.

Bills, Jay, and Shirley Bills. *Home Food Dehydrating: Economical "Do-It-Yourself" Methods for Preserving, Storing & Cooking.* Bountiful, Utah: Horizon Publishers, 1974.

Bone, Eugenia. *Well-Preserved: Recipes and Techniques for Putting Up Small Batches of Seasonal Foods.* New York: Clarkson Potter/ Publishers, 2009.

Brobeck, Florence. *Old-Time Pickling and Spicing Recipes.* New York: Gramercy Pub. Co., 1953.

Brown, Lynda, Carolyn Humphries, and Heather Whinney. *Preserve It!: Bottled Fruits, Jams & Jellies, Pickles, Cured Meats.* New York, N.Y.: DK Publishing, 2010.

Canning, Freezing, and Storage of Foods. Washington, D.C.: U.S. G.P.O., Supt. of Docs., 1987.

Dubbs, Chris, and Dave Heberle. *Smoking Food: A Beginner's Guide.* New York: Skyhorse Pub., 2008.

Greene, Janet C., Ruth Hertzberg, and Beatrice Vaughan. *Putting Food By.* 4th ed. Lexington, Mass.: Stephen Greene Press, 1988.

Hériteau, Jacqueline. *Preserving And Pickling: "Putting Foods By" In Small Batches.* New York: Golden Press, 1976.

Orr, Kathryn J. *Freezing Foods.* Honolulu, Hawaii: Cooperative Extension Service, University of Hawaii, 1972.

Ortiz, Elisabeth Lambert, and Judy Ridgway. *Clearly Delicious: An Illustrated Guide to Preserving, Pickling & Bottling.* London: Dorling Kindersley; 1994.

Parker, E. R. *Economical Housekeeping Complete System of Household Management for Those Who Wish To Live Well at a Moderate Cost : All Branches of Cookery Are Carefully Treated, and Information Given on Canning Fruits, Curing Meats, Making Butter,* Washing, Ironing, Dye. Toronto: J.S. Robertson, 1886.

Peterson, Una Jean W. *Dehydrating: For Food and Fun.* Marysville, Wash.: Golden Sun Productions, 1976.

Reader, Ted. *The Complete Idiot's Guide to Smoking Foods.* New York: Alpha/Penguin Group, 2012.

Ruhlman, Michael, and Brian Polcyn. *Charcuterie: The Craft of Salting, Smoking, and Curing.* New York: W.W. Norton, 2005.

The Complete Guide to Food Dehydrating. 2nd ed. Minneapolis, Minn.: Alternative Pioneering Systems, 1979.

Tinklin, Gwendolyn L. *Freezing foods.* Manhattan, Kan.: Agricultural Experiment Station, Kansas State College of Agriculture and Applied Science, 1963.

Tressler, Donald Kiteley, and Clifford F. Evers. *The Freezing Preservation of Foods,* 3rd completely rev. and augm. ed. Westport, Conn.: Avi Pub. Co., 1957.

Walker, Alison. *A Country Cook's Kitchen: Time-Tested Kitchen Skills : Simple Recipes For Making Breads, Cheese, Jams, Preserves, Cured Meats, And More.* New York: Rizzoli International, 2012.

Weingarten, Matthew, and Raquel Pelzel. *Preserving Wild Foods: A Modern Forager's Recipes For Curing, Canning, Smoking, and Pickling.* North Adams, MA: Storey Pub., 2012.

Apps

How To Can: Ogden Publications, Inc.

If you cannot have your book in front of you, this app will help you in the canning process.

Available for Android and iTunes.

Jam Recipes by Bigo

Nice little app for those wanting to try their hand at jam making. Recipes, podcasts, and more.

Available for Android.

Foods Keeper by Meganeapps

Manage the food that you already have in storage. Sort, search, and "best before" notification. I have found this to be a handy app, but you need to discipline yourself in keeping it updated.

Available for Android.

Jerky Recipes by Bigo

Make your own jerky and save money. Recipes, videos, and podcasts.

Available for Android.

MY HARVEST
JOURNAL

_____

_____

_____

_____

_____

_____

_____

_____

_____

_____

_____

_____

_____

_____

_____

_____

_____

_____

MY HARVEST JOURNAL

_____

_____

_____

_____

_____

_____

_____

_____

_____

_____

_____

_____

_____

_____

_____

_____

_____

_____

MY HARVEST JOURNAL

_____

_____

_____

_____

_____

_____

_____

_____

_____

_____

_____

_____

_____

_____

_____

_____

_____

_____

_____

_____

MY HARVEST JOURNAL